Joyce Appleby on *Thomas Jefferson*
Louis Auchincloss on *Theodore Roosevelt*
Jean H. Baker on *James Buchanan*
H. W. Brands on *Woodrow Wilson*
Alan Brinkley on *John F. Kennedy*
Douglas Brinkley on *Gerald R. Ford*
Josiah Bunting III on *Ulysses S. Grant*
James MacGregor Burns and Susan Dunn on *George Washington*
Charles W. Calhoun on *Benjamin Harrison*
Gail Collins on *William Henry Harrison*
Robert Dallek on *Harry S. Truman*
John W. Dean on *Warren G. Harding*
John Patrick Diggins on *John Adams*
Elizabeth Drew on *Richard M. Nixon*
John S. D. Eisenhower on *Zachary Taylor*
Paul Finkelman on *Millard Fillmore*
Annette Gordon-Reed on *Andrew Johnson*
Henry F. Graff on *Grover Cleveland*
David Greenberg on *Calvin Coolidge*
Gary Hart on *James Monroe*
Michael F. Holt on *Franklin Pierce*
Roy Jenkins on *Franklin Delano Roosevelt*
Zachary Karabell on *Chester Alan Arthur*
Lewis H. Lapham on *William Howard Taft*
William E. Leuchtenburg on *Herbert Hoover*
Gary May on *John Tyler*
George S. McGovern on *Abraham Lincoln*
Timothy Naftali on *George H. W. Bush*
Charles Peters on *Lyndon B. Johnson*
Kevin Phillips on *William McKinley*
Robert V. Remini on *John Quincy Adams*
Ira Rutkow on *James A. Garfield*
John Seigenthaler on *James K. Polk*
Hans L. Trefousse on *Rutherford B. Hayes*
Tom Wicker on *Dwight D. Eisenhower*
Ted Widmer on *Martin Van Buren*
Sean Wilentz on *Andrew Jackson*
Garry Wills on *James Madison*

Zachary Taylor

John S. D. Eisenhower

Zachary Taylor

THE AMERICAN PRESIDENTS

ARTHUR M. SCHLESINGER, JR., AND SEAN WILENTZ

GENERAL EDITORS

Times Books

HENRY HOLT AND COMPANY, NEW YORK

Times Books
Henry Holt and Company, LLC
Publishers since 1866
175 Fifth Avenue
New York, New York 10010
www.henryholt.com

Henry Holt® is a registered trademark
of Henry Holt and Company, LLC.

Library of Congress Cataloging-in-Publication Data

Eisenhower, John S. D., 1922–
Zachary Taylor / John S. D. Eisenhower. — 1st ed.
p. cm. — (American presidents)
Includes bibliographical references and index.
ISBN-13: 978-0-8050-8237-1
ISBN-10: 0-8050-8237-9
1. Taylor, Zachary 1784–1850. 2. Presidents—United
States—Biography. 3. United States—Politics and
government—1849–1853. 4. Generals—United States—
Biography. 5. Mexican War, 1846–1848—Campaigns. I. Title.
E422.E57 2008
973.6'3092—dc22
[B]   20070460783

Henry Holt books are available for special promotions
and premiums. For details contact: Director, Special Markets.

First Edition 2008

Map by Chris Robinson

Printed in the United States of America

1   3   5   7   9   10   8   6   4   2

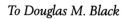

To Douglas M. Black

Contents

Editor's Note

THE AMERICAN PRESIDENCY

The president is the central player in the American political order. That would seem to contradict the intentions of the Founding Fathers. Remembering the horrid example of the British monarchy, they invented a separation of powers in order, as Justice Brandeis later put it, "to preclude the exercise of arbitrary power." Accordingly, they divided the government into three allegedly equal and coordinate branches—the executive, the legislative, and the judiciary.

But a system based on the tripartite separation of powers has an inherent tendency toward inertia and stalemate. One of the three branches must take the initiative if the system is to move. The executive branch alone is structurally capable of taking that initiative. The Founders must have sensed this when they accepted Alexander Hamilton's proposition in the Seventieth Federalist that "energy in the executive is a leading character in the definition of good government." They thus envisaged a strong president—but within an equally strong system of constitutional accountability. (The term *imperial presidency* arose in the 1970s to describe the situation when the balance between power and accountability is upset in favor of the executive.)

The American system of self-government thus comes to focus in the presidency—"the vital place of action in the system," as Woodrow Wilson put it. Henry Adams, himself the great-grandson and grandson of presidents as well as the most brilliant of American historians, said that the American president "resembles the commander of a ship at sea. He must have a helm to grasp, a course to steer, a port to seek." The men in the White House (thus far only men, alas) in steering their chosen courses have shaped our destiny as a nation.

Biography offers an easy education in American history, rendering the past more human, more vivid, more intimate, more accessible, more connected to ourselves. Biography reminds us that presidents are not supermen. They are human beings too, worrying about decisions, attending to wives and children, juggling balls in the air, and putting on their pants one leg at a time. Indeed, as Emerson contended, "There is properly no history; only biography."

Presidents serve us as inspirations, and they also serve us as warnings. They provide bad examples as well as good. The nation, the Supreme Court has said, has "no right to expect that it will always have wise and humane rulers, sincerely attached to the principles of the Constitution. Wicked men, ambitious of power, with hatred of liberty and contempt of law, may fill the place once occupied by Washington and Lincoln."

The men in the White House express the ideals and the values, the frailties and the flaws, of the voters who send them there. It is altogether natural that we should want to know more about the virtues and the vices of the fellows we have elected to govern us. As we know more about them, we will know more about ourselves. The French political philosopher Joseph de Maistre said, "Every nation has the government it deserves."

At the start of the twenty-first century, forty-two men have made it to the Oval Office. (George W. Bush is counted our forty-third president, because Grover Cleveland, who served nonconsecutive terms, is counted twice.) Of the parade of presidents, a dozen or so lead the polls periodically conducted by historians and political scientists. What makes a great president?

Great presidents possess, or are possessed by, a vision of an ideal America. Their passion, as they grasp the helm, is to set the ship of state on the right course toward the port they seek. Great presidents also have a deep psychic connection with the needs, anxieties, dreams of people. "I do not believe," said Wilson, "that any man can lead who does not act . . . under the impulse of a profound sympathy with those whom he leads—a sympathy which is insight—an insight which is of the heart rather than of the intellect."

"All of our great presidents," said Franklin D. Roosevelt, "were leaders of thought at a time when certain ideas in the life of the nation had to be clarified." So Washington incarnated the idea of federal union, Jefferson and Jackson the idea of democracy, Lincoln union and freedom, Cleveland rugged honesty. Theodore Roosevelt and Wilson, said FDR, were both "moral leaders, each in his own way and his own time, who used the presidency as a pulpit."

To succeed, presidents not only must have a port to seek but they must convince Congress and the electorate that it is a port worth seeking. Politics in a democracy is ultimately an educational process, an adventure in persuasion and consent. Every president stands in Theodore Roosevelt's bully pulpit.

The greatest presidents in the scholars' rankings, Washington, Lincoln, and Franklin Roosevelt, were leaders who confronted and overcame the republic's greatest crises. Crisis widens presidential opportunities for bold and imaginative action. But it does not guarantee presidential greatness. The crisis of secession did not spur Buchanan or the crisis of depression spur Hoover to creative leadership. Their inadequacies in the face of crisis allowed Lincoln and the second Roosevelt to show the difference individuals make to history. Still, even in the absence of first-order crisis, forceful and persuasive presidents—Jefferson, Jackson, James K. Polk, Theodore Roosevelt, Harry Truman, John F. Kennedy, Ronald Reagan, George W. Bush—are able to impose their own priorities on the country.

The diverse drama of the presidency offers a fascinating set of tales. Biographies of American presidents constitute a chronicle of wisdom and folly, nobility and pettiness, courage and cunning, forthrightness and deceit, quarrel and consensus. The turmoil perennially swirling around the White House illuminates the heart of the American democracy.

It is the aim of the American Presidents series to present the grand panorama of our chief executives in volumes compact enough for the busy reader, lucid enough for the student, authoritative enough for the scholar. Each volume offers a distillation of character and career. I hope that these lives will give readers some understanding of the pitfalls and potentialities of the presidency and also of the responsibilities of citizenship. Truman's famous sign—"The buck stops here"—tells only half the story. Citizens cannot escape the ultimate responsibility. It is in the voting booth, not on the presidential desk, that the buck finally stops.

—Arthur M. Schlesinger, Jr.

Author's Note

Some years ago, at a dinner at the Smithsonian in Washington, I sat next to a gentleman who seemed to be something of an authority on American history. Our conversation was casual and I must admit somewhat off the subject of the after-dinner speaker. I recall only one remark from our entire exchange, but it was a big one. "In my opinion," my dinner partner said, "there was only one man who, had he lived, might have averted the American Civil War." When I asked the name of the individual he had in mind, he answered, "Zachary Taylor."

To satisfy my curiosity, he went on to explain. "Taylor," he said, "was a southerner, a slaveholder, who opposed the expansion of slavery. He might have been able to talk the language of his fellows from the South and bring some reason into things." But then he added an afterthought. "Of course the Civil War might have come on at that point, a decade earlier."

This was a new picture of Old Rough and Ready, as Taylor was often called, from the one I had formed from my previous writings on Taylor. I had just finished a book on the Mexican War (1846–1848) in which he, along with Winfield Scott and President James K. Polk, was one of the three most important figures on the American side. And yet, though Taylor's military talents were largely recognized by all, he had been pictured as a rough-hewn soldier, practically illiterate, to whom Secretary of War William Marcy had assigned a highly qualified staff officer to write his orders and correspondence and generally "keep him straight." The fact that he was informal in dress and attitude, though endowed with southern courtesy, had convinced me to discount the possibility that he could have been a successful chief executive during the time he lived.

Certain bits of evidence had emerged, to be sure, to introduce disquieting tinges of doubt into my blithe assumptions about Taylor's limitations. Most important was the discovery of a little book reproducing the very sensible letters Taylor wrote during the war to such people as his son-in-law, the surgeon Robert Wood. But I still followed the crowd in downplaying Taylor's importance.

I was therefore delighted when offered the opportunity to take a fresh, broader look at Taylor's career and come to my own conclusions as to what history might have looked like had fate allowed him to serve out his four years as president and possibly go on to a second term. A definite conclusion, manifestly, is impossible, but it is at least entertaining to contemplate how different things might have been had Taylor, and not Millard Fillmore and Franklin Pierce, been at the helm of state between 1850 and 1857.

To make any sort of guess, however, one must examine Taylor's whole life, not merely the confused sixteen months that he was in office. It is the purpose of this small volume to do just that.

Zachary Taylor

1

Early Career

Zachary Taylor was a man whose looks deceived those who met him for the first time. One glance at that rough physiognomy could convince the casual viewer that here was a son of a poor family, a man of the soil. The fact was that Zack Taylor—Old Rough and Ready—was indeed a farmer, but a gentleman farmer. Throughout his life, even when he was in the army, he kept ownership of several plantations, tilled by numerous slaves. His face was weather-beaten, to be sure, but his exposure to the elements came from his time in camp and field, a place where he endured the same hardships as the youngest and toughest of his soldiers.

Taylor was born on November 24, 1784, in Orange County, Virginia, not far from Montpelier, the home of his distant cousin the future president James Madison. His father, Richard Taylor, had served as an officer in the Continental Army during the Revolutionary War and enjoyed the status of being the head of one of the prominent families of Virginia. The Taylors never reached the eminence enjoyed by the Lees and the Carters, but they were a family of respect.

Richard Taylor's outstanding service in the Revolution ironically resulted in Zachary Taylor's leaving Virginia and becoming a Kentuckian. A grateful nation, still governed under the Articles of Confederation, granted Richard Taylor a large parcel of land at a point near Louisville, Kentucky. Richard Taylor accepted, presumably with enthusiasm. The land that comprised his extensive holdings in Tidewater Virginia was beginning to wear out from excessive tobacco raising. Further, they could never compare in size and quality with the land he was being offered in the West. Having determined to move, Richard Taylor began the journey with his pregnant wife, the former Sarah Dabney Strother of Maryland. They soon realized, however, that the journey would be too arduous for her. He therefore left her and their two sons with relatives in Virginia while he headed west alone. He returned seven months later, having cleared some ground near his future homestead. Zachary Taylor, meanwhile, had been born in Virginia. But since he spent only his first eight months there, he could hardly be called a Virginian in the traditional sense.

The Taylors made their way to Kentucky by water, reaching Louisville on August 2, 1785. They settled in their log cabin on Beargrass Creek, five miles to the east of town, on a four-hundred-acre farm they called Springfield. There Zachary, his two older brothers, and yet unborn siblings were to be raised.[1]

Louisville, on the wild frontier, bore no resemblance to the genteel Tidewater district the Taylors had left. Wild animals filled the woods surrounding Springfield, and wild Indians in the vicinity had not accommodated themselves to the invasion of the white man. As a result, young Zachary grew up in an atmosphere where danger was accepted. Sometimes it had its humorous side. A nearby neighbor, Mrs. Chenoweth, seemed to derive some strange pleasure in startling the young people by removing her headgear and displaying her bald head, which was described as "peeled like an onion by the Indians' scalping knife," and "shorn of her beautiful hair."[2] So the story went, though the circumstance of her being scalped is not disclosed.

Zachary Taylor's formal education was scanty, despite the fact that both of his parents were considered upper class. He learned to read and write, of course, like many other isolated children, at "his mother's knee." His first extant letter, in which he accepted a commission in the United States Army, was rough and full of mis-spellings. But given the circumstances of the frontier, his training in farming and taking care of himself was far more important than book learning. He was also, like his father, a shrewd businessman and competent farmer. Throughout his life his properties continued to grow, and his conversation, even in camp, often dealt with agricultural subjects. He was able to accomplish this balancing act because of the peculiar nature of the army at that time. The establishment was scattered in small detachments along the western frontier and except for occasional Indian disturbances was at peace. The authorities, therefore, were generous in granting long leaves of absence whereby an officer could return to his ranch or farm for extended periods of time. Land was wealth, and during his lifetime Zachary Taylor, measured by that standard, became a wealthy man indeed.

Though he was a planter, Zachary Taylor was first and foremost a soldier. The aura of his father's service in the Revolution apparently caught his imagination, and his participation in the various skirmishes with the Indians, while largely unrecorded, seems to have imbued him with a fighting spirit. He was not attracted to fancy uniforms nor to the parade ground, but practical soldiering seems to have become second nature to him. The personal informality was misleading, however; beneath his casual exterior, he was a martinet.

He first joined the army in 1808, at the age of twenty-three, when he applied for and received a commission as a first lieutenant. Taylor was fortunate; normally a young man lacking in formal military experience could never enter service at that rank. It was a troubled time, and the army was being expanded in anticipation of possible war with Britain over the *Chesapeake-Leopard* Affair, in which the crew of a British ship, the HMS *Leopard*, had forcibly boarded the United States ship USS *Chesapeake*, killing three, wounding eighteen, and removing several sailors of British birth. Though President Thomas Jefferson did not resort to war, the tensions and talk of war remained.

On being commissioned, Taylor was assigned to the new Seventh Infantry Regiment, just being organized. It was commanded by

Lieutenant Colonel William Russell, another Kentuckian. The regiment at the moment existed only on paper; to fill its ranks the men had to be recruited. So Taylor began his career as a recruiting officer. He was sent first to Washington, Kentucky, where he found little enthusiasm on the part of the citizenry for military life. He went on to Mayville, where he had better luck.[3] In April 1809, he took his new company of about eighty men by boat from Kentucky to New Orleans.

The situation at New Orleans was hardly conducive to inspiring a young man to remain in military life. The troops were suffering in the heat of the New Orleans summer, and to make matters worse they were commanded by a rogue, Brigadier General James Wilkinson. At a time when rogues abounded, Wilkinson was unique in the varieties of his villainy. Some officers were treacherous, some were avaricious, and some were simply incompetent. Wilkinson managed to combine all three. Perhaps the least of his flaws was his greed. "One of the more senior officers in the Army," writes the historian Edward Coffman, "set an extraordinarily bad example. In the range of his ventures—land speculation, assorted business enterprises, including some of dubious legality, and being a paid agent of Spain—General Wilkinson took second place to none."[4]

At about the time of Taylor's arrival at New Orleans, Wilkinson was about to embark on the project for which he is most infamous. At that time, the bulk of the army, about two thousand men, was concentrated under his command, and the condition of the troops was grim. They suffered from the heat and indulged in the fleshly temptations of the city to the extent that everyone, even Wilkinson, agreed that they had to be moved. Secretary of War Henry Dearborn therefore ordered Wilkinson to move his army up the Mississippi River to Fort Adams, near Natchez, where conditions were said to be relatively healthy. Wilkinson may not have received this order in time because communications were slow. In any case he moved, not to Natchez but to a spot below New Orleans on the Mississippi only thirteen miles away from the city. (It has been assumed that his business interests, plus the allurements of his current mistress, were instrumental in his choice.) The name of the spot was Terre Aux Boeufs, and a worse place could not be found. As aptly described by Taylor's biographer, Holman Hamilton,

Here the general stood by helpless as his troops suffered, sickened, and died. The Kentuckians, who composed the Seventh Infantry and who had undergone the coldest winter in memory, succumbed even faster than their comrades. Conditions at camp beggared description. More men were sick than well, and it was impossible to care for all their needs. Sanitation did not exist. Spoiled food, supplied by seedy and frequently corrupt contractors, revolted those who were supposed to eat it. Attempts at burial were pitiful. Interred higgledy-piggledy in shallow graves, the protruding arms and legs of the deceased took the place of missing markers in reminding the living of the fate that might be theirs.[5]

The story did not end there. When orders finally arrived insisting that Wilkinson's troops be moved to Natchez, the trip by water, involving weakened men, was as deadly as the camp. Nearly the entire army was wiped out. It was one of those rare instances in which an army was destroyed without the firing of a single bullet.

Taylor himself was spared most of the trials of the Terre Aux Boeufs calamity because he succumbed to the prevailing illness early but survived it. He was sent home to Louisville to recover while Wilkinson's army was being rebuilt at Natchez. He took his time back at Louisville in getting his personal holdings in order.

While on this extended leave at Louisville, Zachary Taylor met his future wife, Margaret Mackall Smith, who was visiting her sister, Mrs. Samuel Chew, in nearby Jefferson County. The couple secured their marriage license on June 18, 1810, and three days later were married. In honor of the occasion, Taylor's father presented the couple with 324 acres of land. In the spring of the next year, their first daughter, Ann, was born.[6]

When he returned to duty, Taylor found himself in an entirely different situation from that at New Orleans. The immediate crisis with Britain had passed, and the bulk of the army was now once more spread out across the western frontier, which at that time ran along the Ohio River. This dissipation of force was brought about primarily by the need to protect the civilian settlers against Indian attack. Added to that, however, was the distaste that sophisticated easterners had for the army in general. With memories of the arrogance of the British redcoats of the Revolution, Americans had always held the military with some suspicion. On the other hand, the American people nevertheless recognized the need to maintain a small standing army. Their attitude is well expressed in a letter from Secretary of the Treasury Albert Gallatin to his wife, written in 1802:

> The distribution of our little army to distant garrisons where hardly any other inhabitants is to be found is the most eligible arrangement of that perhaps unnecessary evil that can be contrived.[7]

That deployment, a string of small posts, meant that every fort consisted of perhaps twenty or so men and one or two officers, who were, as mentioned, granted long periods of leave.[8]

Taylor had taken full advantage of this liberal policy of the army, and he went back to duty willingly. At age twenty-six, he was now launched on three careers: planter, family man, and soldier. Try as he would not to neglect any of them, the career as soldier would always take priority.

2

Unsung Hero

When he returned to military duty in early 1811, Captain Zachary Taylor had already attained a reputation for reliability and responsibility, despite the fact that his service had been relatively limited. At the outset he was given a difficult assignment, the command of Fort Knox, Kentucky, a post near Vincennes, Indiana, to straighten out a nasty situation. His predecessor was undergoing a court-martial for allegedly having shot and killed one of his lieutenants, with whom he had quarreled for some time. The situation was symptomatic of the tensions that could arise on the frontier, usually out of sheer boredom. Taylor was the only officer in the area in whom the local commander, Major George Clark, had confidence to restore order.

Taylor reestablished discipline quickly but was not to remain long in command. After he had been only a month at Knox, unexpected orders arrived, sending him to Frederick, Maryland, where he was to testify as a witness in a court-martial. General James Wilkinson was being tried for misconduct at Terre Aux Boeufs, and for some reason he thought that Taylor's testimony would help his case. Taylor was never actually called to the stand, however, probably because his testimony was not needed. Wilkinson had enough friends in high places that, as with his other courts-martial, he was acquitted and restored to command. Taylor returned to recruiting duty at Louisville.[1]

That period of idleness deprived Taylor of participation in a major event, for while he was at Frederick, William Henry Harrison, the governor of Indiana, fought the much-touted Battle of Tippecanoe against the forces of the legendary Indian leader Tecumseh. The battle itself was not the shining victory that was later portrayed in Harrison's political campaign literature. His force of one thousand regulars and volunteers marched north from Vincennes to destroy the village of Prophetstown, the domain of Tecumseh's brother. On November 7, 1811, at the point where the Wabash joins Tippecanoe Creek, Harrison's men walked into an ambush set by a congregation of four hundred Indians.[2] Harrison's tough frontiersmen rallied and finally drove off the attackers. Having done so, they proceeded to burn Prophetstown. The action, though unduly expensive in American losses, was lavishly celebrated by the public, and even when the truth became known, the legend was already too firmly implanted to be discredited. Nearly thirty years later its aura would carry Governor Harrison into the White House. Missing that battle meant Taylor's missing a chance to make a name for himself.

Tippecanoe was a relatively small battle, and the burning of an Indian village in itself was of little consequence. Nevertheless, it was significant in that it made undying enemies of the Indians, who might have been ambivalent in choosing which was the lesser of two evils, the Americans or the British, who were energetically wooing them. Tecumseh stepped up his depredations against American villages, thus creating a public perception that the British in Canada were encouraging Tecumseh and his tribesmen to drive the settlers out of the area. Though the official justification for the American declaration of war against Britain in June 1812 was the British impressments of American seamen, involving as it did an insufficient acceptance of the United States as a full-fledged nation, the British fomenting of Indian unrest also played a major role.[3]

Taylor's big moment in the War of 1812 came very early. In March 1812, before the actual declaration of war, he had been ordered to take eighty men, women, and children, mostly men, to Fort Harrison, a critical outpost on the eastern bank of the Wabash River north of Vincennes. As Taylor's contingent was on the way, they were struck by disease; only fifty-six men and nine women and children eventually made it to the fort.[4] Even after settling into the garrison, the members of the party did not quickly recover. As late as September the vast majority of them were still sick with fever. Taylor himself was just recovering from some mysterious disease called "bilious fever," for which we today have no explanation. By one account, only a dozen men were free from disease, and only two sergeants and four privates could mount guard at a time.[5]

When Taylor arrived at the fort, he was told that the local Indians had been outwardly quiet recently, and for the time between Taylor's arrival and early September they remained so. However, any complacency that existed among the garrison was eventually erased when two young farmers outside the fort were killed, scalped, and mutilated. Taylor buried the bodies near the fort and from that time on kept an elevated alert despite the poor physical condition of his troops.

On the night of September 4, 1812, a figure was seen approaching the fort. It turned out to be an Indian named Joseph Lemar, with whom Taylor was familiar. The visitor was bearing a flag of truce and was followed by a band of forty people, some of them women. The local chief, Lemar said, would come to the fort the next morning to discuss how the Americans could provide some food to help his people, who were suffering from starvation.

Taylor instantly sensed treachery. Asking for food was an old trick, and he and his men could recognize among Lemar's entourage Winnebagoes, Kickapoos, Pottawatomies, Shawnees, and some Miamis, tribes that were known to be from northern Indiana, the area of Prophetstown. Additionally, some friendly Miamis warned Taylor of potential foul play. The proposed parley never came to pass.

That night Taylor and his men went to sleep fitfully, and just before midnight they were awakened by the sound of fire from the sentries. All of Taylor's men, except the very sickest, assumed their assigned stations against an attack by hundreds of Indians. It soon became apparent, however, that the attack was halfhearted, and its objective was the blockhouse. The fort was a log structure, designed according to the standard of the time. It was square, with two sentry posts on opposite corners and the all-important blockhouse along one of the walls. The Indian leaders, familiar with such forts, knew that the building held all the supplies for the garrison. In a short period of time a couple of braves managed to set the blockhouse on fire.

As the fire began to spread, the situation became an emergency. Taylor could see that the blockhouse was at the critical point, and he devoted his attention to it. Confusion nearing panic engulfed the garrison, and two of Taylor's men who were in robust health leaped the walls and deserted. But here, as described by the historian Benson Lossing, Taylor's leadership exerted itself:

> Nothing saved the fort but the presence of mind, courage, prudence, and energy of the commander. The fire was about to communicate to the barracks, when he shouted, "Pull off the roofs nearest the blockhouse, pour on water, and all will be well." His voice gave courage to his troops. Water was brought in in buckets, and several of the men, led by Doctor Clark, climbed to the roof, cut off the boards, and by great exertions, in the face of bows and arrows, they subdued the flames, and saved the menaced buildings. Only eighteen or twenty feet of the fort was opened by the fire.[6]

Once the fire was brought under control, Taylor directed his men to build a temporary breastwork to fill the gap, and by dawn the structure was as high as a man's head. With the approach of daylight the Indians gave up the attack and pulled back. From then on, they contented themselves with slaughtering all the livestock in the vicinity and watching the fort from a respectful distance. Fortunately for Taylor and his men, the Indians did not burn all the corn that was just ripening in the farmlands outside but protected by the fort. For several days, therefore, the defenders of Fort Harrison subsisted on corn that was not quite ripe. It may not have been tasty, and it may have caused some upset stomachs, but the garrison survived.

Danger persisted, however, and it was only on September 12, a week after the battle, that Taylor judged it reasonable to send two messengers into the darkness to take a message to Vincennes. Three days later the two soldiers gave Taylor's report to the acting governor of Indiana, John Gibson. In the meantime, however, Colonel William Russell, still commanding the Seventh Infantry, decided on his own to come to Taylor's rescue. He took twelve hundred men and reached Fort Harrison at about the same time as Taylor's messengers reached Gibson.[7]

Taylor was generously recognized for his action at Fort Harrison. Not only did Colonel Russell congratulate him warmly but also Governor Gibson. General Samuel Hopkins, from Taylor's home state of Kentucky, referred to "the firm and almost unparalleled defence by Captain Z. Taylor." The action was written up in Eastern newspapers.

The most remarkable of Taylor's honors, however, came from President James Madison himself. On October 31, 1812, the *Intelligencer* announced that Captain Zachary Taylor had been awarded the rank of brevet major. It was the first brevet ever awarded in United States history.[8] The rank involved no raise in pay, and the authority that went with it was questionable. The brevet system later came under severe criticism, but for Taylor it was a signal honor.

· · ·

Though Taylor was probably unaware of it, his success at Fort Harrison represented the first victory attained by the American armed forces since the outset of war the previous June. Small outposts throughout Wisconsin and Minnesota had fallen to combined forces of British and Indians. These losses were minor, however, compared to those suffered by the American garrison at Detroit just before the Fort Harrison defense.

On August 15, 1812, General William Hull, governor of the Michigan Territory, had abjectly surrendered his army of one thousand men at Detroit, thus destroying all the ambitious plans the Americans had been conjuring up for the conquest of Canada. The American public reaction was severe, and Hull was actually sentenced to death for cowardice. That sentence, palpably too severe, was soon mitigated, partly because Hull had performed with gallantry as an officer in the American Revolution.

A major result of Hull's removal and disgrace was that William Henry Harrison, whose scope had previously been limited to the Indiana Territory, was now placed in command of all the American forces in the West. At the same time, Taylor's reputation, indeed his newfound fame, brought him added responsibility. Soon after the action at Fort Harrison, he was assigned as aide to General Samuel Hopkins, a position which at that time amounted to that of a chief of staff. But recognition did not bring with it rapid promotion. Circumstances were responsible: the western theater was a sideshow compared to operations on Lake Ontario. It was not generally realized in Washington that Taylor's defense of Fort Harrison had actually brought Indian aggression in the Indiana Territory to a halt. Tecumseh, the tribe's leader, had withdrawn his forces to the north, where they could operate with the British.

Not so in northern New York. On October 12, 1812, an American force under General Stephen Van Rensselaer was repulsed in an effort to cross the Niagara River into Canada at Queenston. A good many of Van Rensselaer's men were captured. Operations on the New York front became so active that all attention was henceforth focused on that area. Taylor recognized that fact and made efforts to be transferred to the eastern theater of war. In that, however, he was unsuccessful.

Defensive operations in the West continued but proved to be frustrating. The American objective after Fort Harrison was to consolidate the frontier of the Wabash. General Hopkins, with Taylor assisting him, led a force of two thousand militia in an attempt to destroy a Kickapoo village along the Illinois River. The expedition completely failed, partly because of supply shortages and lack of forage (which were real) but primarily because of a lack of zeal on the part of the green troops. Hopkins was forced to give up the enterprise and retrace his steps back to Vincennes. But since it was still only November, Hopkins and Taylor mounted one more expedition. From Vincennes they marched northward along the Wabash, past Fort Harrison, and up to Prophetstown, where they destroyed some Indian villages. Though men were lost in skirmishes, no pitched battle occurred.

At this point, Taylor's fighting activities came to a halt that lasted all through 1813. He spent some time recruiting in the Indiana Territory and then took some sick leave at home in Louisville. While at home he continued applying for a transfer to the eastern theater. When that effort failed in July, he returned to command at Fort Knox, where he remained the rest of the year, even bringing his family to join him. The lack of a stern fight was by no means Taylor's choice; the Indians—and the war—had simply gone to other theaters.

In the spring of 1814 Taylor was called back into active service. The War Department had now turned its attention to the Mississippi River and was bolstering the western defenses against the British and Indians. For a while Taylor was in temporary command of all troops in the Missouri Territory, with headquarters in St. Louis, but was soon superseded by Brigadier General Benjamin Howard. The two men were concerned over the possibility of a British sweep down the Mississippi to take St. Louis. Their fears were reinforced by the fact that two American outposts, one at the junction of the Mississippi and Rock rivers and the other at the outpost of Prairie du Chien, had been overrun by British and Indians.

Howard decided that the best defense was to attack. He therefore planned to lead an expedition up the Mississippi to the Rock River to burn a cluster of villages, a tactic that remained for years the standard army way of fighting the elusive Indians. Once that part of the mission was achieved, he planned to retrace his steps and build a fort near the juncture of the Mississippi and the mouth of the Des Moines River. Before the expedition could get under way, however, General Howard fell sick with a fever and was unable to go. He was determined, however, that the venture should proceed anyway, under Taylor's command.

Fortunately, Howard was precise, and he gave instructions that made Taylor's later decisions easier.

> Major Taylor will ascend the Mississippi as high as the Indian Villages at the mouth of the Rock River . . . and destroy the villages. He will, after effecting or failing to effect the object at that place, drop down to the Des Moines and erect a fort which must be maintained until further orders can be sent.[9]

Taylor left St. Louis in August 1814 with a force of 430 militiamen and rangers, carried in eight fortified keelboats. He pushed them hard. When the winds died down, he ordered them to take to the oars. He himself led the expedition in the first boat, using a previously prepared chart.

At first all went well, but unforeseen troubles soon began. Many members of Taylor's command came down with the measles, greatly reducing efficiency. The water was shallow in places, and because of the heavy loads of supplies, many of Taylor's men were nearing exhaustion before ever seeing an Indian.

It was September 4 before the Taylor expedition reached the Rock River, and at that point Indians began to appear, some of them crossing the river to the rear. They showed no inclination to parley but at one point attempted a clever ruse: they released a large number of horses on Credit Island in the middle of the river, inviting the Americans to try to catch them. Taylor did not fall for that trick. It was an old one.

The rest of that day involved heavy fighting, buffeted by high winds; to shelter his fleet from the gale, Taylor camped for the night on a small, willow-covered island just north of Credit Island. By the next morning, heavy fighting resumed, and Taylor began a counterattack. It met with success and soon Taylor's men had cleared Credit Island of Indians. A surprise then hit: the Indians were joined by a force of thirty British redcoats under the command of British lieutenant Duncan Graham with a three-pounder gun, manned by an expert gunner.

Here is where Howard's discretionary orders came into play. Taylor, outnumbered three to one and faced with Graham's lethal artillery piece, went through the motions of a council of war, in which he decided to retreat. Once out of the area of Credit Island and the Rock River, Taylor's force was no longer molested. As a compensation for what might be called a defeat, no hostile British and Indian forces ventured south of Credit Island again.

As Howard had specified, Taylor built a fort at the juncture of the Des Moines and Mississippi rivers, which he named Fort Johnson. In late October, however, Taylor was called back to St. Louis upon the death of General Howard. Rather than leave the fort intact for the enemy to use, he destroyed it. He returned to St. Louis. The War of 1812 was over for Zachary Taylor.[10]

With no pressing duties to perform, Taylor turned his attention to righting what he considered a wrong that had been done to him in the matter of promotions. Though he had held positions of responsibility and had been acclaimed as the defender of Fort Harrison, he was still a captain, with a brevet to major. Granted, Taylor had spent a good deal of time commanding garrisons such as Fort Knox in which there was little danger, but too many officers commissioned after him had been promoted to permanent major, and he determined to do something about that.

There were possible explanations for the slight—or perceived slight. One was the strange system of promotion by regiment rather than from a single list comprising all the officers of the army. An officer who was serving in a regiment in which vacancies occurred might be promoted faster than one of his contemporaries in a regiment with more stability.

Taylor suspected another cause, the enmity of two officers of higher rank who bore great animosity toward him, Colonel William P. Anderson and Anderson's assistant, Captain W. N. Wilkinson. Their enmity apparently stemmed from Taylor's disobeying orders by ordering Lieutenant Joseph Perkins to leave recruiting duty in April 1814 to accompany William Clark, the governor of the Missouri Territory, in establishing Fort Shelby at Prairie du Chien. This affront to Anderson's dignity, necessary as it was, caused him and Wilkinson to send floods of letters to Secretary of War James Monroe castigating Taylor.[11]

Taylor took the bull by the horns and in late November 1814 he wrote the adjutant general requesting information on the effect of these complaints against him. At the same time, he enlisted the support of several friends, some of them prominent, to write on his behalf.[12]

The pressure apparently worked. In January 1815 the adjutant general wrote Taylor that "no complaints had been made" to damage his good reputation with the War Department.[13] And soon Taylor's promotion to major in the regular army came through.

Unfortunately for Taylor's career, the War of 1812 had ended by the time the adjutant general's letter arrived, and on March 1, 1815, Congress reduced the army from sixty thousand men to ten thousand. Taylor, having so recently attained his full promotion, was to be reduced to the grade of captain once more. He was not being discriminated against. The new organization consolidated four regiments into one, and of the twelve majors in the regiment, only three, including Taylor, were to be retained in the service.[14]

That compliment—which it really was—did not suffice for Zachary Taylor. He journeyed to Washington to plead his case once more. Again rebuffed, he refused his commission when it was offered on June 15, 1815, and he retired to Louisville to take up a new life as a farmer, supposedly with no regrets.

3

Old Rough and Ready

Back at his plantation in Louisville, Taylor at first welcomed his return to the soil. "I have commenced making corn and tobacco & am now in my own cabbin [sic]," he wrote to a distant relative. "I do not," he added, "regret the change of calling or the course I have pursued."[1]

Cheery words such as those soon began to fade, however, as the routine life of a gentleman farmer wore thin. After a few months Taylor was writing in a different vein: "[My life] affords me nothing sufficiently interesting to trouble my friends by communicating with them on the subject."[2]

Rescue from ennui came to Taylor after he had been home less than a year. Two vacancies in the grade of major occurred in the Third Infantry, and Taylor was offered one of them. He accepted the offer and was mustered back into service on May 17, 1816. By coincidence, Margaret Taylor gave birth to their third daughter, Octavia, on the same day as an order arrived instructing Taylor to report to General Alexander Macomb, commanding the Fifth Military District at Detroit.[3] Taylor took his time in reporting, and it was a full four months after receiving his orders that he arrived in Detroit. There he was given command of Fort Howard, a new bastion under construction in Green Bay, Wisconsin. For the moment Fort Howard was the most important post on the frontier because it was located on the very edge of settled territory. Green Bay was a far cry from Louisville, which was by now boasting paved streets and other accoutrements of civilization. The vast bulk of the civilian inhabitants around Fort Howard were French, mostly rough men with Indian wives or mistresses. They did not welcome the more regulated life that came with the presence of a fort, but given no choice they accommodated.

Taylor's time at Green Bay was apparently uneventful since records are scarce. It could not, however, have been very happy. Whether his wife and daughters joined him is unknown, though Margaret was such a conscientious helpmeet that tradition has held that she was present at least part of the time. In any event, what records have survived tell mostly of difficulties. In common with many other strong commanders, Taylor was a stern disciplinarian with his troops but was often recalcitrant in dealing with his superiors. General Macomb, with whom he never got along, was no exception. Taylor's tour at Fort Howard extended for twenty-two months, and in the summer of 1818 he was granted a furlough to return to Louisville.

Taylor remained in Louisville for a year, during which time several significant events occurred. One was his welcome promotion to lieutenant colonel, which he received on April 20, 1819. A more exciting event took place a couple of months later, when President James Monroe made a journey to visit the western outposts of the army, accompanied by Major General Andrew Jackson, who was then in command of the Western Department. At Frankfort, Kentucky, the party was lavishly entertained, and Zachary Taylor, who had retained a certain aura for his defense of Fort Harrison, was invited to join them. One president and two future presidents were in that room, though nobody realized it, of course. Jackson was showing signs of developing presidential ambitions, but Taylor was the most unlikely presidential prospect imaginable.[4]

A year after that heady experience, in February 1820, Taylor and his family separated again. Officers on the frontier spent much of their time away from home, so it was not considered unusual for

Taylor to place his wife and four daughters in the care of Margaret's sister, Mrs. Samuel Chew, at Bayou Sara, Louisiana. Taylor then joined the Eighth Infantry, which was engaged in building the Jackson Road at a point 125 miles northeast of Madison, Louisiana. From that arduous duty he went on to a series of varied and usually short-term assignments.

During that period tragedy struck. The climate at Bayou Sara was not salubrious, and in July 1820, only five months after the family's arrival, Mrs. Taylor and all four of her daughters came down with malaria. Taylor hastened to his wife's bedside, not expecting her to survive. Margaret, as it turned out, pulled through, though with her health permanently impaired. Not so fortunate was the cherished three-year-old, Octavia, who died.

Hardly had Taylor returned to his station at Bay St. Louis but he received news that the baby of the family, little Margaret, had also died of the disease.[5] The grief from losing two children in the course of four months was not unusual on the frontier, but it was nevertheless devastating. It could well be that this series of tragedies convinced Taylor that military life, with its long separations, was unsuitable for families. No daughter of his, he resolved, would marry an army officer.

The decade between 1820 and 1830 saw Taylor performing standard duty for the army on the frontier. Though still a lieutenant colonel, he commanded the First Infantry from 1832 on; he did not attain his full colonelcy until 1836, and then only after exerting considerable pressure on persons in high places. These adventures in army politics, along with his positions on various boards of inquiry, ensured that Taylor developed some idea of Washington and its ways.

· · ·

In the summer of 1832, along with such future luminaries as Abraham Lincoln, Jefferson Davis, Albert Sidney Johnston, Robert Anderson, and Winfield Scott, Zachary Taylor participated in what came to be called the Black Hawk War. It was a badly handled affair, and Taylor always considered it unnecessary. Nevertheless its roots were real; perhaps it was inevitable.

For years the Sauk and Winnebago Indians on the upper Mississippi frontier had been relatively quiescent, conducting only occasional raids against small groups of whites. They had good reason for many of the raids. The whites had been increasingly moving into their territory in violation of treaties going back to 1804, aided by the fact that the Indian braves were customarily absent from their homes during the winter hunting seasons.

In the early 1830s, however, the Sauks, who occupied the region of Illinois north and northwest of Rock Island, began to turn rebellious. The leader of the discontent was a sixty-five-year-old Sauk chief, Black Hawk, who was determined to stop this thievery; he had had enough.

Black Hawk was a towering figure in the mold of the earlier Tecumseh, whom he resembled in fervor.[6] He presented a striking appearance—reputedly tall and exceedingly thin, with a high forehead and piercing eyes. His hatred of the white man was intense. Black Hawk did not enjoy a universal following among the Sauks; a younger man by the name of Keokuk was in favor of accommodating the whites. But Black Hawk could muster enough followers to put up a significant resistance.

The so-called Black Hawk War lasted only three months—May, June, and July 1832. The trigger was Black Hawk's determination to recover lands extracted from his people in early 1831 by Major General Edmund P. Gaines, commanding the army in the West. Having put down a minor rebellion that year, Gaines had secured from Black Hawk a promise to move his people permanently to lands west of the Mississippi River. Gaines, however, made a serious error in believing that the unrest had been quelled. He had returned to St. Louis leaving only two companies of troops at Fort Armstrong, on Rock Island, a totally inadequate force.

In April 1832, Black Hawk, back home from the annual hunt, had found the treaty again violated and in response decided to cross the Mississippi with a band of fifteen hundred Sauks, one thousand men, women, and children and five hundred braves. From a point near Rock Island they began moving slowly up the south bank of the Rock River, heading northeastward. In so doing, Black Hawk expected to spark a general uprising of discontented Sauks and other tribes to join him. It is also possible that he expected no white reaction so long as his band committed no acts of violence.

The American army's indecisive response, in Taylor's view, was the reason that there was a war at all. General Gaines and the rest of the regulars wanted no part of coming to the rescue of Illinois settlers again so soon. Gaines therefore assigned Brevet Brigadier General Henry K. Atkinson to move up and take charge at Rock Island. Atkinson showed little more zest for the task than Gaines, and he did nothing for a while. Taylor, his principal regular army subordinate, was highly critical of Atkinson's dilatory actions. He observed,

Had the garrison of Fort Armstrong [Rock Island] been reinforced as it could, and ought to have been, with three or four companies from Jefferson Barracks the moment the Mississippi was clear of ice, which was the last of March, there would have been no Indian war.[7]

In mid-April 1832, Atkinson was forced to act. Spurred by news of fresh massacres and by the pleas of Illinois governor John Reynolds for federal troops, he finally moved to Fort Armstrong with six companies of the Sixth Infantry. It was too late: Black Hawk had already begun moving up the south bank of the Rock River.

The ensuing campaign was almost entirely a militia matter. Under Atkinson's overall command, a force of Illinois militia, led by Governor Reynolds, started out with three regiments in pursuit of Black Hawk. Taylor, with three hundred regulars, some militia, and supplies, followed by boat on the Rock River. Atkinson did not accompany Reynolds; instead he accompanied Taylor.

In the first pitched battle of the Black Hawk War, the militia suffered a disaster. Reynolds sent Major Isaiah Stillman ahead with a detachment of Illinois mounted troops, expecting that the force would be enough to subdue Black Hawk. Stillman overtook Black Hawk at a place called Stillman's Run.[8] Black Hawk attempted to surrender but, by a misunderstanding, some trigger-happy militiaman killed two or three of his emissaries. Black Hawk, therefore, decided to go down fighting and attacked with a force of only fifty braves. Stillman was no warrior. He and his men turned and fled the twenty miles back to Reynolds's camp, with a loss of a dozen men, mostly rear guard. As a result, Black Hawk's triumphant warriors ravaged the countryside with raids that caused panic to spread.

Atkinson, his first effort a failure, ceased active operations for the moment. To help build up his force, he established a fort at a place called Dixon's Ferry, on the Rock River, and placed Taylor in command. The fort was to serve as a base from which troops and supplies could be sent to various parts of the territory. Taylor had his hands full because Black Hawk, newly emboldened by his success at Stillman's Run, now began raiding the white settlers all over the territory. It has been estimated that two hundred settlers were killed during this period. Taylor attempted to send various detachments to stop this marauding but met with some difficulty.

At one point, Taylor had the unusual experience of having his orders directly disobeyed. One evening in late May a brigade of newly recruited militiamen arrived at Fort Dixon, exhausted after a long march. Taylor may have sympathized, but he was never prone to spare his men when important missions were in the offing. Since the garrison at Galena was in dire need of reinforcement, Taylor decided to send them on. Realizing that the order would be unpopular, he gave it his all.

You are citizen-soldiers and some of you may fill high offices, or even the presidency some day, but never unless you do your duty. Forward March![9]

The commander of the brigade, however, intervened. Turning to his men, the officer addressed them directly: "You need not obey his orders. Obey mine and follow me." Taylor was in no position to enforce his will. It would be unnatural, however, if the incident had not augmented Taylor's lifelong distaste for militia and volunteers.

By Monday morning, June 25, 1832, Atkinson was ready to resume his campaign. He had gathered a force of twenty-five hundred men, five hundred of them regulars. Black Hawk, with only five hundred braves, had no choice but to try to make his escape back across the Mississippi. He had to turn north to do so; the Rock River, to the south, was solidly held by the whites. It was not easy for Atkinson to locate Black Hawk in that expanse, but the wily Indian chief could not escape forever. In mid-July, he was found and attacked at a place called Wisconsin Heights. In the ensuing battle, sixty-eight of Black Hawk's men were killed.[10] The rest escaped and the pursuit continued.

On August 2, Black Hawk's depleted ranks finally reached the Mississippi and attempted to cross it at the mouth of the Bad Axe Creek, Wisconsin. A firefight broke out, which quickly degenerated into a slaughter. Some of the braves begged for mercy and some may have received it. But most perished. Holman Hamilton estimates that twenty-four white men were killed or wounded, but more than three hundred Indians were killed on the east bank or drowned in the river attempting to escape. Beset by hostile Sioux on the west bank, half of the survivors died at the hands of fellow Indians. Only fifty Indians lived to surrender to the army, one of whom was Black Hawk, who gave himself up at Prairie du Chien on August 27.[11]

Black Hawk, now a prisoner, was placed in Taylor's custody until later turned over to General Winfield Scott, who had just arrived and was now the senior officer. The two young officers who took immediate charge of Black Hawk were Robert Anderson, who would later surrender Fort Sumter to the Confederates in April 1861, and Jefferson Davis, the future president of the Confederacy.

And what effect did Zachary Taylor's participation in the Black Hawk War have on him? Nearly every aspect was unfavorable. Principally, circumstances prevented him from doing much if any fighting. The upper echelon of the military, considering this a state problem, limited the role of the regulars largely to setting up a base and providing logistical support. Taylor, nearly excluded from actual fighting, was thus denied any opportunity to earn promotion to the brevet rank of brigadier general, which he craved.

Perhaps more important for Taylor's future as a commander of both regulars and volunteers was the growing distrust that Old Zack was developing toward all volunteer troops. He wrote letters to both Scott and Major General Thomas Jesup on the subject, blowing off steam, but never recovered from his bias.

• • •

The year 1832 held one more significant event for Zachary Taylor, this one of a personal nature with strange and tragic results. It had to do with Lieutenant Jefferson Davis and his intense romance with Taylor's eldest daughter, Sarah.

Sarah, eighteen years old, may not have been a classic beauty, but she was handsome, vivacious, and strong-willed. Her swain, born in Kentucky, was a West Point graduate from the class of 1828 and currently a member of the Second Dragoons. Eight years her senior, he was a responsible young man, as demonstrated by his having been put in charge of Black Hawk earlier in the year.

There was no doubt in the minds of either of the young lovers that they intended to marry, but they ran afoul of the iron will of the young lady's father. Taylor had never lost his determination that no daughter of his would ever marry an army officer.

An impasse resulted and with it grew a personal animosity between Zachary Taylor and Jefferson Davis. Davis was forbidden to enter the Taylor quarters, and the lovers were forced to resort to elaborate schemes just to meet. In March 1833, the situation was temporarily relieved when a promotion to first lieutenant in the

First Dragoons led to a series of new assignments for Davis in the Southwest, a hiatus that lasted a full two years. In their absence from each other, however, the two maintained such an intense relationship by correspondence that when they met again nothing of their feelings for each other had been lost.

In June 1835, Davis sent in his resignation as an officer in the United States Army. That act should have cleared the air for a reconciliation between him and Taylor, but for some reason that did not occur. So, when Davis and Sarah were married on June 30, the wedding took place at the home of Sarah's aunt Elizabeth near Louisville.

There was, unfortunately, to be no happy ending. Leaving Louisville after a large family wedding, the newlyweds took a steamer down the Mississippi to visit Davis's elder brother Joseph. There, in early August, both Sarah and Jefferson contracted malaria, and soon Sarah died. Death came suddenly and unexpectedly. Apparently still feeling well, she wrote a last cheerful letter to her mother asking that she convey her "love to Pa."

It was the great tragedy of Taylor's life; Jefferson Davis went into seclusion from which he did not recover for a long time.

• • •

In Taylor's long service on the western frontier, there were inevitably long periods in which little transpired of any interest to history. Relief from the sameness occurred when he received orders, in late 1837, to proceed with a considerable force from Missouri to Florida to participate in the open sore called the Seminole War.

The Second Seminole War was one of the least noted and yet costliest and most frustrating "wars" the United States Army ever fought against the various Native American tribes. One general after another failed to bring the Seminoles to their knees. Careers would have been shattered had not all the other prominent generals encountered failure as well. The problem had not been the strength of the stubborn Seminoles but their elusiveness.

The most spectacular failure had been that of Brigadier General Winfield Scott, the army's perennial and usually successful troubleshooter, who conducted a major operation in early 1836, shortly after the massacre of a contingent under Major Francis L. Dade, for whom the county of Miami, Florida, was named.

With several regiments of South Carolina, Georgia, and Florida volunteers, Scott organized three columns, one from Fort King (Ocala), one from Cape Canaveral, and one from Fort Brooke (Tampa), to converge on a supposed Seminole strongpoint on the Withlacoochee River, west of Gainesville on Florida's west coast. After much difficulty, the three wings met, not at the Withlacoochee but at Tampa in early April 1836. By that time the terms of service of the volunteers had expired, and the campaign had reluctantly been abandoned. It was a spectacular and expert military operation, but it encountered few Indians: they had simply melted into the landscape.

A later commander, Thomas Jesup, had besmirched his name in the minds of many by white man's treachery. He had called a truce with the charismatic Seminole leader Osceola and, while the Indian leader was under a white flag, seized him and dragged him off to Fort Moultrie, South Carolina, where the poor man died under suspicious circumstances a month after his incarceration.[12]

Jesup was still in command when Taylor arrived at Fort Gardner with 1,000 men, a command that included 180 Missouri volunteers, a small group of "Morgan's Spies," 70 Shawnee Indians, and the First, Fourth, and Sixth Infantry Regiments. His area of operations, under Jesup, was to be in southern Florida, starting from the Kissimmee River toward the Everglades. In December 1837, Taylor requested and was granted permission to move out against some bands of Seminoles in that area.

At first Taylor's force met with success. Small bands of Seminoles surrendered to his men and were sent back to the various forts he was constructing along the way as he moved south. A remarkable feature of these surrenders was the fact that some of the captives were longtime antagonists toward the Americans and toward each other. They included the famed Jumper (Ote Emathla), one of the band that had participated in the Dade massacre in December 1835.

On Christmas Eve 1837, Taylor's force approached the Seminole line, one of the rare defensive positions the Seminoles ever established. It had been organized well, placed behind a swamp about three feet deep with water and mud. The grass concealing the position was five feet high, and the grass had been cut to allow for the defenders to lay down defensive fire. The weakness of the position was that it was held by three independent groups, each under a separate chief. Coacoochee commanded on the left, Alligator in the center, and Sam Jones on the right. Of the 380 to 480 warriors, Sam Jones commanded about half.[13] None of these chiefs would take orders from the other, so the Seminoles lacked a coordinated command.

Just after noon, on a beautiful Christmas day, Taylor's men moved out. His tactics are open to debate. He sent his least experienced troops, the Missouri volunteers, out ahead of his main body as a skirmish line, this over the protests of their commander, Colonel Richard Gentry, who thought the position could be flanked. Once the skirmish line had identified the enemy position, Taylor committed his main body, the Sixth Infantry on the right and the Fourth on the left. He kept the First Infantry in reserve. All went directly forward through the swamp, Taylor himself through muck up to his waist.

Not all went well at first. The Sixth Infantry on the right ran into stiff resistance, and its regimental commander was mortally wounded, as was Gentry of the volunteers. But the weak position in the Seminole line, the right under Sam Jones, began to give way, at which time Taylor committed the First Infantry to roll up the enemy flank from that direction.[14]

There was not much of a flank to roll up. Once the Seminoles saw that their cause was lost they simply disappeared into the Okeechobee swamp to their rear. The field—and therefore the victory—was Taylor's. But at a cost. The Americans had lost 26 killed and 126 wounded. The Seminoles, 11 killed and only 14 wounded.

The significance of the Battle of Okeechobee was mostly psychological. As one of the rare pitched battles of the Second Seminole War, it received much attention throughout the United States. Some of it was controversial. Taylor accused the Missourians, who had lost almost nobody but Colonel Gentry, of cowardice. The Missouri press and politicians accused Taylor of sacrificing his militiamen to save his regulars. But Secretary of War Joel Poinsett backed Taylor to the hilt. Taylor succeeded to the command in all of Florida, where he suffered the same frustrations as his predecessors. His two years there constituted the longest term for any of the succession of army commanders in the peninsula.

His time in Florida earned Zachary Taylor two things. One was promotion by brevet to brigadier general and the other, based on his personal bravery in advancing through the Okeechobee swamp with his men, was the bestowal of the nickname Old Rough and Ready.

4

Fort Jesup to the Rio Grande

Taylor remained in Florida until April 1840. By that time he was tired and pessimistic about prospects for really settling the Seminoles. He asked for relief, which was reluctantly granted, and returned with his wife to New Orleans and Baton Rouge after a long trip to Washington and the East Coast—a form of "rest and recreation." He was also granted a substantial leave to get his affairs in order. In his long absence, his plantations were encountering financial difficulty, and they needed his personal attention. He was then assigned to command at Fort Gibson, Oklahoma, the headquarters of the region and the last stop of the tragic "Trail of Tears," the removal of the Cherokees from Georgia to new homes west of the Mississippi.

Early in 1841, Taylor stepped out of character for a moment by showing an interest in politics, or at least politicians. The newly inaugurated president William Henry Harrison, his old commanding officer from the War of 1812, had just entered the White House, and Taylor made contact with him and expressed views critical of the "corruption" of the Andrew Jackson administration and the "ineptness" of the administration of Jackson's successor, Martin Van Buren. The correspondence led to nothing, for Harrison survived only a month in office. Nevertheless, this was the first occasion in which Taylor had identified himself as a member of the Whig party.[1]

Taylor settled down in the Southwest, always agitating to be assigned as close as possible to Baton Rouge, and he succeeded in being transferred from Fort Gibson to Fort Smith, Arkansas. For the next three years, he kept peace on the frontier with little of note transpiring.

In early June 1845, Taylor received orders from Washington to amass a small force of two infantry regiments and part of a dragoon regiment at Fort Jesup, Louisiana, on the Sabine River across from Texas. Taylor had no problem with this move; he was familiar with the troops—the Third and Fourth Infantry Regiments and the Second Dragoons—and even more so with Fort Jesup. He had, in fact, established that outpost himself some fifteen years earlier, naming it after the army's quartermaster general, Thomas Jesup, one of Taylor's staunchest supporters. What Taylor could not foresee was that this seemingly routine military move would eventually lead him to the White House.

Taylor may have seemed to be an unlikely choice for this field command, the largest concentration of regulars since the Revolution. Other potential candidates were higher ranking. Winfield Scott, the general-in-chief of the army, was the obvious choice. Another possibility could have been Edmund Gaines, commanding the Western Division, in which Taylor's operation was to occur. But both of these officers, bitter rivals to each other, were confirmed members of the Whig party. Scott had, in fact, declared himself available for the presidency as early as 1839. Taylor did not carry that albatross. Former president Andrew Jackson had advised the current chief executive, James K. Polk, that in case of war with Britain over the Canadian border issue, Taylor should be the man to lead the American forces. Jackson's recommendation probably reflected some of his personal animosities toward Winfield Scott, but it carried weight.

Taylor's force, called the Army of Observation, was being sent to Fort Jesup ostensibly to protect the Texans from any interference from Mexico as they debated whether or not to accept an American invitation to join the Union, an invitation that might well bring about war with Mexico. His future role, however, was more significant. He was to move to the western border of Texas when so advised by the American chargé d'affaires in Texas, Andrew Jackson "Jack" Donelson.

Whether Texas would accept the invitation to join the Union was never in doubt. For ten years the status of Texas as an independent country had always been precarious. Raids across the Texas-Mexico border had occurred at various intervals, and it was always possible that Mexico might make one more effort to recapture its wayward state. Despite the reservations of Texas president Sam Houston, who could not oppose annexation in public, the desires of the people were pronounced. Donelson and Taylor therefore decided that Taylor could jump the gun and move to the tiny village of Corpus Christi a couple of weeks before the formal vote of July 4.

Although Taylor's force was small—only two infantry regiments and part of the Second Dragoons—shipping to transport it was tight. Only one regiment could be sent by steamer at a time. Taylor therefore decided to send the Third Infantry aboard the steamer *Alabama* and to accompany it personally. The Fourth Infantry would follow in sailboats. As a show of force, at Donelson's request, Taylor sent the Second Dragoons, under Colonel David Twiggs, overland. The dragoons would meet up with the infantry at Corpus Christi.

Once Twiggs had left, Taylor took a civilian steamer from Fort Jesup to New Orleans. On board, he spotted a man who looked familiar; it turned out to be Jefferson Davis, his son-in-law a dozen years earlier, with whom he had been on hostile terms. No hostility remained. When the two men introduced themselves, Davis disclosed that he was on the way to Natchez to marry a Miss Varina Howell. Taylor wished him the very best for future happiness. It seemed as if the suffering they had previously shared now stood as a bond between them. From then on, though their politics would differ, they would behave almost like father and son.

The selection of Corpus Christi as the place for Taylor's army was fraught with political significance. With Texas joining the Union a foregone conclusion, the question still remained as to the boundary between Texas and Mexico. The Mexicans contended that the boundary ran along the Nueces River; the Texans, however, claimed an additional strip of land 150 miles wide, placing the border on the Rio Grande. The area between the two rivers became disputed territory.

Despite the bulk of other opinion, Polk sided with the Texans. Therefore it was significant that the village of Corpus Christi was situated on the right (south) bank of the Nueces River, in the disputed area. Though nearly all of Polk's officers felt they were intruding in Mexican territory, the president held to his position; however, he did not advertise it.

In early July, Taylor accompanied the Third Infantry as it marched down the streets of New Orleans to board the *Alabama*, the Fourth Infantry not far behind. The voyage took three weeks, and the *Alabama* reached Aransas Bay only on July 25, 1845. The Third Infantry, the first to arrive, encountered a great deal of difficulty because of the shoals off the Nueces River. Once on dry land, however, Taylor's men were in their element. The army adhered to a standard procedure for setting up camp. The Fourth Infantry soon arrived, and the beach at Corpus Christi was adequate to hold the entire command. Eventually it grew to a strength of 3,550 officers and men. When the time approached for David Twiggs and the Second Dragoons to arrive, an impatient Taylor took a small party and headed inland toward the Mexican town of San Patricio to meet him. That act was typical of Zachary Taylor. The average commander would stay at camp in his comfortable tent and send out a patrol to report to him. Not Taylor; he went himself.

Taylor may have regretted his impatience. His guide lost his way, and Taylor had to spend another uncomfortable night sleeping on the ground. The next day, however, Twiggs and the Second Dragoons arrived at San Patricio a little ahead of schedule. Twiggs had heard noises from the direction of Corpus Christi and had mistaken thunder for artillery fire. In his mind, he was coming to Taylor's rescue. The date was August 24, 1845.

Life in camp started out quietly enough, and morale was good. Taylor's men, veterans of the American frontier, were accustomed to camp life away from their families, if they had any, and the Army of Occupation, as it was now called, boasted a third of the entire regular army.

Taylor had never expected to stay long at Corpus Christi, considering it a way station to Matamoros on the Rio Grande. He was held up, however, by President Polk's attempts to negotiate the purchase of a vast area now known as the American Southwest from the Mexican government, which had no desire to sell it for any price. So, while they were all stuck on the beach of the Nueces, Taylor seized the opportunity to train his army. Although Taylor's officers and men were tough, self-reliant, and reliable as individuals and in small groups, they had never maneuvered, much less fought, as units larger than companies. Colonel Ethan Allen Hitchcock, a former commandant of cadets at West Point, claimed to be the only officer present who had ever commanded a regiment as a single unit. The Army of Occupation now had an opportunity to whip itself into shape. It was small, granted, but its newfound efficiency would make it a match for a force far greater than its size.

This period of relative inactivity was perhaps the one in which Taylor himself could best be observed by his subordinates. He seemed content to take it easy and await developments. George G. Meade, a lieutenant in the Topographical Engineers and the future victor at Gettysburg, kept a careful diary of the time and he recorded his observations of Taylor. Taylor, he wrote, was

a plain, sensible old gentleman, who laughs very much at the excitement in the Northern states on account of his position, and thinks there is not the remotest possibility of there being any war.

And then Meade added,

He is said to be very tired of this country, and the duty assigned to him, and it is supposed will return [to his plantations] on the arrival of General [William] Worth.

To top it all off, Meade echoed the rumor that Taylor, as a purported Whig, was totally opposed to the annexation of Texas.[2]

There was no question that Taylor was informal in his manner and dress. He almost never wore a proper uniform, and on one occasion, according to a questionable source, a young lieutenant came by his tent to "see the general." The general apparently absent, he approached an old man cleaning a saber and offered his new friend a dollar to clean his own. The young man returned the next day to retrieve his saber, only to discover that "Old Fatty," as he had called the gentleman, was the general himself—who also said, "I'll take that dollar."[3]

Not everyone viewed Taylor benignly. Hitchcock, commanding the Third Infantry, believed that beneath this informal, disarming behavior, Taylor was actually nursing a strong ambition. When Taylor casually mentioned the idea of "going to the Rio Grande" one day, Hitchcock, in his diary, called it "singular language for one who originally and until very lately denounced annexation as both injudicious in policy and wicked in fact." Taylor, he opined, "wanted another brevet and would strain a point to get it."[4]

For some months the Army of Occupation followed a normal garrison routine on the beach at Corpus Christi. The temperature was salubrious at first and even with the drilling the duty was not harsh. Numerous leaves were granted for hunting expeditions, and the countryside provided plenty of game. Firewood to cook the animals they bagged to supplement their rations was somewhat scarce, but it could always be found. The health of the command was good, except for mild diarrhea from the slightly brackish water the men were forced to drink. As late autumn came on, however, spirits began to sag. The nights became chilly and boredom set in. Corpus Christi swelled with camp followers, including some women of dubious repute. One officer was court-martialed for getting into a fight over a woman. In everyone's mind, it was time to move on.

One individual with hopes of a quick departure was Lieutenant Meade, and he was elated when he was designated to head a reconnaissance party down to the mouth of the Rio Grande to inspect a harbor called Brazos Santiago, presumably the future base of supply for the army when it arrived at Matamoros. When Meade's orders were canceled, he surmised, correctly, that the move was off. The army would stay at Corpus Christi for the winter.

In late November an incident occurred that served as evidence of shortening tempers. For one of the few times in his tenure as a commander, General Taylor scheduled a review of the Army of Occupation. Quite conceivably Taylor was using the device to restore a sense of discipline in his troops, who were becoming sloppy. It seemed to be a good idea.

The planning hit a snag, however. As the commanding general, Taylor would of course be the reviewing officer, but who would command the troops as they passed in review? There were two candidates. One was Colonel William J. Worth, Taylor's second in command, and the other was Colonel David E. Twiggs, of the Second Dragoons. Worth was a colonel on the regular promotion list who had also been awarded a brevet to brigadier general. Twiggs had no brevet to brigadier but ranked higher than Worth in regular rank. Which was to take precedence, regular or brevet rank? For some strange reason, even though Taylor himself had been awarded the first brevet for his action at Fort Harrison thirty years earlier, the War Department had never really defined what it meant, that is, whether the honor of the rank carried with it the authority of the rank. Probably the question had never arisen before because individuals receiving brevets were likely senior in regular rank as well.

Taylor selected Twiggs, opting for the precedence of the regular list over brevets. The issue split the army. So hot did feelings become that a group of officers, led by Hitchcock, sent a round-robin to the United States Senate to protest the decision. In the meantime, a disgusted Taylor canceled the review. Though the issue was no longer immediate, Washington's decision was still a matter of interest. It was an example of the mischief that the whole concept of brevets could perpetrate.

• • •

Despite the undesirable conditions at Corpus Christi, Taylor's Army of Occupation was forced to remain in place while President Polk pursued his ends through diplomatic means. He was willing to fight to attain his goals, the annexation of California and what was then called New Mexico,[5] but he preferred, quite naturally, to do so by purchase rather than war.

To that end, Polk sent an emissary, John Slidell, to Mexico, armed with a series of proposals for various purchases. For example, if Mexico would agree to a boundary along the Rio Grande, ceding half of New Mexico, the United States would assume Mexico's outstanding debts to the United States and pay $5 million. For a boundary that would include all of New Mexico and Upper California, to include the city of Monterey, California, the United States would pay $25 million.

Mexico, however, still refused to sell any of its land at any price, and President José Joaquin de Herrera even refused to receive Slidell. On Christmas Eve 1845, Slidell fired off a bitter message to the Mexican government and retraced his steps to Veracruz. He eventually returned to Washington in a rage. With that failure, Polk felt free to pursue his objectives by provoking a war. On January 13, 1846, therefore, Polk instructed Secretary of War William Marcy to order Taylor to the Rio Grande.

Taylor received his order happily; he had long recommended the move. Marcy's order admonished Taylor not to initiate hostilities with the Mexicans unnecessarily, but it allowed him to judge for himself if the Mexicans had done so. In other words, the president was delegating the choice of war and peace to a field commander. The order also authorized Taylor to call on the governor of Texas to reinforce him with such militia as "may be needed to repel invasion or to secure the country against apprehended invasion."[6]

Taylor took the order in his own good time. He would go when he was ready. He reinstituted plans for scouting parties to canvass the route to Matamoros and to inspect the conditions at Brazos

Santiago as a possible base. He also decided that his main body—three infantry brigades and the Second Dragoons—should arrive at Matamoros at the same time as his sea component, which was carrying supplies and equipment. He refused, however, to send the vessels carrying the supplies without naval protection. A hostile vessel could practically destroy his invasion by sinking the ships carrying his supplies.

Taylor appealed to Secretary Marcy in Washington to secure him naval protection, but he didn't receive it. At first the request was refused or delayed. Then a couple of unseaworthy vessels were produced. The situation was at a stalemate. Taylor's problem was solved by a phenomenon not uncommon in the military services. Help came locally. Commodore David E. Conner, commanding the navy's Home Squadron on the East Coast, heard of Taylor's problem and came to his rescue, supplying a couple of adequate gunboats and placing them under Taylor's command.

Taylor had one other decision to make, whether to call on the governor of Texas for militia reinforcements. For the moment, at least, he decided not. Time was short, and Taylor always preferred to keep as high a percentage of regulars in his army as possible. He would take only his original Army of Occupation. After all the delay, it was March 8, 1846, before Taylor's advance guard—Twiggs's Second Dragoons and the light artillery of the army—left Corpus Christi.

Taylor's order of march was predicated on the assumption that he would meet no stiff Mexican resistance before the Arroyo Colorado, a large gully about thirty miles north of Matamoros. Accordingly, he sent out one brigade per day. The First Infantry Brigade, under General William Worth, left the encampment on March 9, the Second Brigade on March 10, and the Third Brigade on March 11. Taylor himself remained behind at Corpus Christi to see the Third Brigade off. Then, by riding thirty miles a day, he planned to catch up with the First Brigade at about the time it reached the Arroyo Colorado. As always, Old Rough and Ready rode like any other officer, with no special shelter. His lips were dry and cracked yet, at age sixty-one, he showed no unusual fatigue. Nor did he mention any discomfort in his dispatches back to Washington.

Matamoros lies considerably to the west of Corpus Christi, so Taylor's route was eased by his marching a good bit of the distance up the Nueces River. The trail to Matamoros was well marked, and as anticipated no resistance was met until the Second Dragoons and the First Brigade reached the Arroyo Colorado. There, on the south bank, stood a cavalry force of Mexicans looking as if they were ready for a fight. Twiggs, who had arrived earlier, had found that there was no place to cross the abyss without meeting resistance.

On the next day, March 20, the Second Brigade arrived, and Taylor believed that he was strong enough to force the issue without awaiting the arrival of his Third Brigade. He placed the Second Brigade on the right of the First and ordered a frontal charge.

Down the banks of the arroyo the two brigades went, with the band playing "Yankee Doodle." The flamboyant William J. Worth insisted on leading the charge on horseback. Once the Americans reached the far bank, however, they found the Mexican cavalry gone. The Battle of the Arroyo Colorado was over almost before it began. Some of Taylor's officers and men found the whole episode an exciting experience. Taylor, however, found it undramatic. "The crossing was then commenced and executed in the order prescribed," he reported to Washington, and added, "Not a shot was fired."[7]

For the last thirty miles to the river, Taylor kept his army intact but found the precaution unnecessary; no more Mexican resistance appeared. When the lead troops reached a road junction at the bank of the river downstream of Matamoros, Taylor's principal concern for the moment was to ensure that his future supply base at Point Isabel, at the Brazos Santiago, would be secure. Accordingly, he left General Worth in command of his three infantry brigades with instructions to find a suitable camping ground short of the final destination. In the meantime he personally accompanied Twiggs by turning left to Point Isabel. Worth camped at a pond called Palo Alto.

At Point Isabel, Taylor was delighted with the scene that greeted him. All three vessels, the two gunboats provided by Conner's Home Squadron and the supply ship of the army quartermaster, had arrived.[8] The only ominous note came from clear evidence of Mexican intent. One of the buildings had been burned down and somehow a leaflet signed by the Mexican commander was found, sounding a call to arms to all Mexicans. Not unexpectedly, Taylor's Army of Occupation was not to be greeted with a welcome mat.

Taylor rejoined Worth on March 28, and the united army began the march upstream to find a point across the river from Matamoros. It had marched nearly 150 miles over sandy terrain, sometimes in intense heat without water, in seventeen days. It was an impressive feat. But then Taylor's were exceedingly tough men.

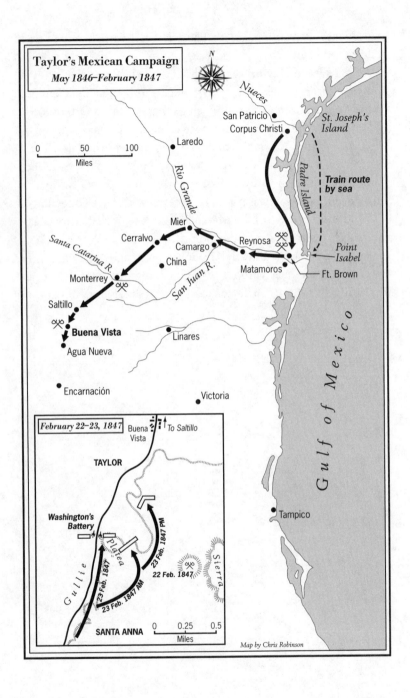

Taylor's Mexican Campaign
May 1846–February 1847

N

Nueces

San Patricio
Corpus Christi

St. Joseph's
Island

Laredo

0   50   100
Miles

**Train route
by sea**

Rio Grande

Mier

Cerralvo

Camargo

Reynosa

Point
Isabel

Santa Catarina R.

China

San Juan R.

Matamoros

Ft. Brown

Monterrey

Saltillo

Buena Vista

Linares

Agua Nueva

Padre Island

Encarnación

Victoria

Gulf of Mexico

February 22–23, 1847

Buena
Vista

To Saltillo

TAYLOR

**Washington's
Battery**

Plateau

23 Feb. 1847 PM

23 Feb. 1847

23 Feb. 1847 AM

22 Feb. 1847

Sierra

Gullie

23 Feb. 1847

SANTA ANNA

0   0.25   0.5
Miles

Tampico

Map by Chris Robinson

5

War with Mexico!

When Taylor's army reached the Rio Grande, they peered across the hundred-yard stream for a glimpse of the Mexican town of Matamoros. If they expected the banks of the river to be filled with curious spectators, however, they were disappointed. The banks were lined with armed sentries, and behind them the town was festooned with Mexican flags, but civilians were scarce. The Mexicans had prudently pulled all the small boats over to their side of the river.

At first the Mexicans showed little hostility. In the afternoon, in fact, a group of young women emerged from behind the line of sentries and came down the bank of the river. They disrobed in front of the spectators on both sides and plunged into the water for a swim. A few American officers who were already in the river swam toward them. The Mexican sentries on the opposite bank let the Americans reach almost to the middle before letting it be known that they were to go no farther. The young officers blew kisses to the tawny damsels, who laughed and returned the compliments. Both groups then swam back to their respective shores.[1]

After that playful little episode, however, any evidence of friendliness disappeared. Taylor waited until afternoon, then decided to open communications with Mexican general Francisco Mejía, whom he knew to be in command at Matamoros. To represent him,

Taylor sent Worth, in whom he had confidence to handle things well. Worth went to the riverbank displaying a white flag. Soon the Mexicans sent a boat to take him over to their side of the river.

Nothing went well. Mejía refused to talk with anyone but Taylor, requiring Worth to transact his business with Mejía's second in command. No matter. The two soon came to a clear agreement to disagree. The Mexicans demanded that the Americans leave the left bank of the river, which they insisted was part of the Mexican state of Tamaulipas. They did not yet consider the two countries to be at war, but they refused to allow Worth to see the American consul in Matamoros. Before returning to the American side, Worth stated forcefully that the Americans would stay where they were. It was certain now that hostilities would break out sooner or later, but when?

Tensions grew rapidly. The Mexicans did not wait for nightfall before starting to build a breastwork and installing a twelve-pound cannon, pointed at the Americans. Not to be outdone, Taylor placed an artillery battery aimed straight at the building known to be General Mejía's headquarters. At the same time his engineers began to construct an elaborate redoubt. That was all the hostile action at first.

A few days later an unfortunate incident occurred. A message from President Polk laid down a final ruling regarding the precedence of brevet versus regular rank. Regular rank was to be given precedence. Worth, who had taken a stand otherwise back at Corpus Christi, regarded the ruling as a personal affront. He took informal leave of Taylor and departed, declaring his intention to resign from the army.

Taylor deeply resented Worth's departure. He expressed his feelings in a revealing letter to his son-in-law Dr. Robert Wood; beneath his facade of Southern courtesy and manner, there lurked a nature that could be judgmental, even vindictive. Worth, he wrote, had been pampered and bloated for "things he never done or acts he never performed." Then, the final insult from a man who led his troops from the front:

There are few if any officers in the service who require more from the private soldier to make himself comfortable, or who would put himself to less inconvenience for their benefit.[2]

. . .

For a while after Taylor's arrival, things remained quiet for his army. The most serious problem was the tendency for some of his discontented soldiers to desert. The troops had been away from civilization for a long time, and the authorities at Matamoros had made the most of that fact. They gave royal treatment to a couple of dragoons who had crossed the river on a lark, and the men reported the incident to their comrades. Many of Zack's enlisted men were foreigners, principally Irish and German, who felt little patriotic fervor for an America that had refused to accept them as full-fledged citizens. Some men, particularly Irish, succumbed to the siren song that Mexico was a Catholic country and it was wrong for Catholics to fight Catholics. The desertions were not numerous enough to weaken Taylor's army to any great extent, but it was not a desirable situation.

On April 9, a little less than two weeks after Taylor's arrival, the army was shocked when the quartermaster, Lieutenant Colonel Truman Cross, disappeared from camp. Cross was a popular officer, and many officers and men, on their own, went out to search for him. His body was found about a week later, at the same time as that of a young lieutenant, David Porter.

Taylor did not regard these hostile acts as representing official Mexican policy, however, especially since a notorious Mexican renegade, Antonio Canales, was known to be in the vicinity. In addition, Taylor knew that the Mexican garrison of Matamoros was insufficient to pose much of a threat to him. That situation changed, though, when Francisco Mejía was replaced by a red-headed forty-three-year-old officer named Mariano Arista, who came at the head of some three thousand troops. Arista had been sent to Matamoros for the sole purpose of destroying Taylor's army, and he was eager to do just that. On April 26, Arista sent a cavalry detachment of sixteen hundred men across the Rio Grande at a point some miles upstream of Taylor's position. There they waylaid an American patrol that Taylor had sent to investigate. Sixteen Americans were killed; the rest, including its commander, Lieutenant Seth Thornton, were captured.

This was it. Taylor sent a message back to Washington: "Hostilities may now be considered as commenced."

• • •

On Friday, May 8, 1846, President James Polk met with his cabinet in the White House considering what to do next regarding Mexico. Word had not reached him of the action on the Rio Grande, but his emissary, John Slidell, had just arrived back from Veracruz. Polk, ever single-minded, regarded President Herrera's refusal to meet with Slidell as a national insult.

Up to this time, Polk had been restrained by a controversy with Britain over the disputed boundary between Canada and the United States, running west of the Great Lakes to the Pacific. For years the two countries had delayed facing the problem by jointly occupying the vast Oregon territory. In the meantime both sides had been indulging in a great deal of posturing; indeed some of Polk's supporters in the 1844 presidential election had howled the jingoistic slogan "Fifty-Four Forty or Fight," threatening war if Britain did not concede all the Oregon territory. The fuss was needless. Neither country wanted war; they were tied together too closely economically, and the foreign ministries of both countries had long been counting on a boundary running due west from its origin—that is, along the 49th parallel of latitude. Now Secretary of State James Buchanan was nearing an agreement with the British along those lines, with the United States conceding the entire island of Vancouver. Though the final agreement had not yet been signed, President Polk was confident that he could discount the threat of war with both Britain and Mexico. He could now concentrate on Mexico.

Based on the treatment that Slidell had received in Mexico, Polk believed he had justification for war. He polled his cabinet and found that two very important members had the audacity to protest against initiating war. One was Secretary of State James Buchanan and the other was Secretary of the Navy George Bancroft.

The next day, Saturday, Polk and his cabinet met again. This time Polk managed to browbeat Buchanan into agreeing to a declaration of war. Polk then overrode Bancroft and announced that three days hence, on Tuesday, he would send a war message to Congress.

That evening Polk's problem vanished. Taylor's message from the Rio Grande arrived, announcing that hostilities had commenced; therefore no urging of Congress was necessary. Polk and his staff worked over the weekend composing a war message that had as its core the premise: "American blood has been shed upon American soil." The message included a subtle shifting of the blame for Taylor's dangerous situation from Polk's shoulders onto those of the general. His earlier orders, Polk asserted, had authorized Taylor to call on the governor of Texas for additional troops, but the general had not availed himself of that opportunity.[3]

The reaction of the House of Representatives was instant. After only a half hour debate, it approved Polk's position that war already existed, by a lopsided vote of 173–14.[4] The Senate took a little longer because the war was opposed by two influential senators, John C. Calhoun and Thomas Hart Benton. Nevertheless, on Wednesday, May 13, the Senate supported the war with a vote more lopsided than that in the House: 40–2. The Congress then went on to approve all that Polk had asked for and more. He was authorized to raise a force of "any number" of volunteers up to 50,000 to serve for a year or "to the end of the war." It was not that the members of Congress were in favor of the war; they were forced to act because Taylor's army was deemed to be in dire danger. No legislator would dare to withhold a penny of the nation's resources to rescue him. At the same time, the anger against Polk was widespread and severe; it was generally—and correctly—thought that he had manipulated the war despite the will of the American people.

. . .

Taylor's position on the Rio Grande was dangerous, if not precarious. An army of fewer than three thousand men could hardly be expected to pose a threat to a nation of seven million people, which was the population of Mexico, and, if not reinforced with competent troops, his army could hardly be expected to hold out indefinitely. His plan, therefore, was simply to hold his position until the expected reinforcements should come and then decide when he could take offensive action.

A major problem lay in the fact that the American force was split between two positions, one across the Rio Grande from Matamoros and the other, Taylor's base, at Point Isabel, thirty miles away. By no means could the road be left open between the two, so each would have to be strong enough to defend itself without the aid of the other.

On May 1, Taylor was satisfied that Fort Texas, as his new bastion was called, could repel any attack the Mexicans might reasonably be expected to launch from Matamoros. He therefore felt free to march back to Point Isabel, leaving Fort Texas in the hands of only the Seventh Infantry, four hundred men, under the command of Major Jacob Brown.[5] The fort had two weeks' rations, more than enough, Taylor believed, to allow him to return with substantial supplies from Point Isabel.

Taylor's men were glad to be on the march, eager to meet the enemy in battle. They were confident of their ability to win a victory, and they would not feel utterly comfortable until they had done so. They had another, intangible incentive: their pride in the regular army. They knew that their ranks would soon be swelled with volunteers. This battle would be fought by regulars alone.

Taylor himself was not the cool, relaxed man that he usually showed the world. He had good reason. His scout, Captain Sam Walker of the Texas Rangers, reported that Arista, still south of the Rio Grande, was moving downstream, perhaps intending to cross the river and cut off Taylor's army before they reached Point Isabel.

So Taylor pushed his men hard, covering thirty miles in less than twenty-one hours over rough terrain.[6] They arrived at Point Isabel at noon on May 2 and immediately began the task of fortifying the position.

Three days after Taylor had arrived, Sam Walker reported that the Mexicans had begun bombarding Fort Texas heavily. Nevertheless, Walker reported, only one man had been killed at the time he had left. Arista's army was now north of the river.

Taylor pondered this news but decided to remain at Point Isabel to complete the fortification. Then, on the morning of May 7, he gave the order to mount up to leave. Taylor expected a battle, and his order was unusually dramatic for him. Delivered by his trusted aide William W. S. Bliss, it concluded:

[The general] wishes to enjoin upon the battalions of Infantry that their main dependence must be in the bayonet.[7]

Taylor's route ran along the Point Isabel–Matamoros road, on which he marched seven miles the first day. The next day, after a total march of eleven miles, his army approached the wide, sandy plain on which was the pond of Palo Alto, Worth's camping ground six weeks earlier. Taylor's scouts reported that the Mexican infantry was drawn up in a double line a mile in length. It was here that the battle would be fought.

The Battle of Palo Alto, fought on May 8, 1846, does not appear to today's observer as much of a fight. There were no dashing infantry charges and very little change in the front lines throughout the day. Taylor, much outnumbered, did not feel free to attack. The Mexican position was too strong, with both flanks protected. Therefore, Taylor decided to deploy his troops at a point seven hundred yards from Arista's position. On the way he ordered his men to fill their canteens, half of them at a time.

Taylor felt no pressure; Arista was showing no signs of making an attack despite his two-to-one superiority in infantry. When Taylor was finally in line, he placed his heavy eighteen-pounder guns in the center of his five infantry regiments with his four light artillery batteries interspersed. On the right flank he placed Major Sam Ringgold's battery and on the left Captain James Duncan's. Taylor himself watched the battle sitting sidesaddle on the back of his faithful mount, "Old Whitey."

Taylor's vulnerable spot was his supply train, three hundred wagons and hundreds of mules and oxen, which carried the food and ammunition he had gone back to Point Isabel to attain. He could not afford to risk them. To compensate for that weakness, he made use of an overpowering new weapon called the flying artillery, of long range and accuracy. Techniques for handling the piece had been developed principally by Ringgold himself. Whereas the Mexican artillery, lacking explosive projectiles, bounced its iron balls on the ground in front of the lines, Taylor's artillery tore holes in the Mexican ranks.

During the day, Arista twice sent General Anastasio Torrejon's sixteen hundred cavalrymen to hit Taylor's vulnerable supply train. Twice Torrejon was intercepted, principally by Ringgold's artillery battery; indeed, after the first attempt, Torrejon's men were so discouraged that they made only a feeble effort the second time.

The Mexican cavalry attacks resulted in a slight change in positions. Ringgold, intercepting Torrejon, pulled his battery out ahead of the previous line, and the infantry followed to give him protection. The change was of little consequence, and when a fire broke out in the chaparral that impeded visibility for both sides, the two armies called it quits for the day. The losses were one-sided in favor of the Americans, but Arista had not been budged from his strong position.

Despite the lack of decisive maneuver, the battle of May 8 had been more important than either side realized. Most of the results were psychological. Taylor realized, almost for the first time, the tremendous value of his flying artillery, which he had discounted up to then, since it had not been of much value in fighting Indians. It is ironic that of the very few American losses, Sam Ringgold, the architect of the decisive weapon, was mortally wounded by a bullet through his thighs. He died a few days later at Point Isabel, probably unaware of the magnitude of his contribution in developing the light artillery.

Even more important, perhaps, was the effect of the battle on the morale of Arista's troops. Forced to stand and take heavy casualties from the American artillery fire, they realized that their own supporting arm was well-nigh useless.

The two armies faced each other on the field of Palo Alto throughout the night. It was particularly miserable for Arista's men because so many of their comrades were lying out on the field moaning. To make matters more uncomfortable, the brushfires had not quite gone out, casting an eerie glow to the night. Early the next morning Arista decided to abandon his position and fall back along the Matamoros road, perhaps hoping that Taylor would not follow him. If he so hoped, he was to be disappointed.

That day, May 9, showed Taylor at his best as a commander. On learning of Arista's departure from Palo Alto, he called a council of war to discuss whether to follow or to remain in place. There were good arguments for the latter course of action. Arista's army, while damaged, was far from destroyed, and it still outnumbered the Americans by two to one. Taylor's army had ample supplies, and they could remain at Palo Alto indefinitely pending the arrival of the reinforcements that Taylor had requested twelve days earlier from Texas and Louisiana. Of the ten officers Taylor had consulted, seven voted for staying in place.

Such a tactic, however, was not Taylor's style. After hearing out the views of his subordinates, he announced, "Gentlemen, you will prepare your commands to move forward."

Arista, who had attained a substantial head start, was able to establish a position six miles behind his original line at a dried-up bayou named the Resaca de la Palma. His deployment seems strange. The Resaca constituted an obstacle, but Arista spread his army out so thinly along its rear side that his advantage in numbers of infantry was of little use. On the north, from which direction

Taylor was coming, he placed an outpost line. The only mobile part of his army was his cavalry. Having put his troops in their places, Arista went back to his sumptuous tent to rest.

When Taylor arrived at the Resaca in the early afternoon, he hoped to be able to repeat his tactics of the previous day and fight an artillery duel. However, he was prevented from doing so because the thick chaparral, worse than that of the previous day, virtually blocked any view of the enemy. Even infantry would be almost impossible to control under those circumstances. Taylor therefore planned to confine his attack to the Matamoros road, where his way was blocked by a Mexican artillery battery. Taking the battery under artillery fire was impossible, so he would charge it with a troop of dragoons under Captain Charles May. In the meantime, a Mexican cavalry attack by Torrejon against Sam Ringgold's old battery, now commanded by Randolph Ridgeley, was repulsed.

Taylor's instructions to May resembled those of the Light Brigade at Balaklava only a short time later. May was simply to charge and capture the Mexican guns on the road ahead. In the meantime, Ridgeley identified the battery's position by lobbing a shell in its vicinity, which the Mexicans foolishly answered back. May was a dashing, unpopular officer but of unquestioned bravery. He charged down the road, jumped the artillery pieces, and made many captures. His triumph, however, lasted only for a moment. Hemmed in by Mexican infantry, he turned his troops back and returned to Taylor's lines.

Taylor was now aroused. Turning to Colonel Belknap, of the Eighth Infantry, he barked, "Take those guns and by God keep them." Belknap moved forward and stormed the position, capturing the guns and the Mexican general la Vega to boot. The rest of the Mexican line, seeing the heart of their position rent asunder, collapsed. It was every man for himself all the way back to the Rio Grande. The lucky fugitives were able to swim across the river to Mexico, but the unlucky ones drowned. Taylor sent a message to the adjutant general: "Our victory has been complete."

For the two days of battle, Taylor listed American losses as 34 killed and 113 wounded. Mexican losses were difficult to estimate, but Taylor claimed 300 killed. He had buried 200. Lieutenant George G. Meade, less modest, claimed 1,200 Mexicans killed in battle, 300 drowned, and between 1,000 and 2,000 deserters.[8]

Taylor followed Arista along the Matamoros road all the way to the river. On entering Fort Texas, he was happy to learn that casualties among the garrison were light. He was saddened, however, to learn that the commander, Jacob Brown, had been killed on the morning of May 5. Taylor renamed the bastion Fort Brown. Its remnants still remain in the town that bears its name, Brownsville.

6

Monterrey

Back in Washington, President Polk and General Winfield Scott were agreed on at least one thing, their strategy against Mexico. Both men visualized occupying her northern states on the theory that doing so would persuade Mexico to agree to a peace on Polk's terms. To reinforce that move, they had long planned to send a force of dragoons and Missouri volunteers under Colonel Stephen Kearny to occupy Santa Fe, New Mexico. If that expedition went well, it might be possible for Kearny to continue from there on to California.

They had come to this agreement despite their mutual animosity. Polk resented Scott's great size, overbearing manner, and somewhat patronizing ways. In addition, Polk knew that Scott had been a national hero ever since the War of 1812 and was a far more popular figure with the American public than was he. Polk's main complaint against Scott, however, was political; the general was an active Whig, a presidential candidate as far back as 1839 and very actively pursuing the Whig nomination for the presidential election of 1848. Admittedly, all the army's top generals were Whigs—besides Scott there were Zachary Taylor, John E. Wool, and even Adjutant General Roger Jones. None of those men were, however, active candidates for the presidency. Only Scott had openly thrown his hat in the ring.

Polk's animosity toward his generals created a painful problem for him. As commander in chief, he could never be seen as wishing any of them ill in fighting their country's battles. However, he dreaded the thought of the laurels that any field commander would inevitably reap for an overwhelming victory. The only answer to the dilemma was to see that whatever general won a victory should receive as little credit for it as possible. To that end, Polk determined to keep Scott in Washington as long as possible. And yet, in the face of public opinion, he could not do so forever. On May 23, 1846, however, that situation changed. Word of Zachary Taylor's triumphs at Palo Alto and Resaca de la Palma arrived. Public opinion now demanded that Taylor remain in command of the army on the Rio Grande. Polk had every logical reason to keep Scott out of trouble in Washington.

· · ·

In the meantime, Taylor, on the Rio Grande, was facing his own set of troubles. Foremost of these was the problem of how to cope with eight thousand unwanted volunteers that Edmund Gaines had recruited from Alabama, Mississippi, Missouri, and Louisiana.[1] Their very numbers strained Taylor's resources. Furthermore, the volunteers, while patriotic and enthusiastic, were untrained, unruly, and anxious for action. But immediate operations were totally unrealistic. Some, of necessity, were therefore simply left to sleep on the beach at Brazos Santiago, whence they had disembarked.

The details of Taylor's future conduct of the war on the Rio Grande were left completely to his own judgment. The only instructions he had received were vague, contained in an order of the previous January: "You will not remain completely on the defensive." Nevertheless, Taylor found little difficulty in sensing that the authorities in Washington desired him to invade Mexico. Therefore, once he had ascertained that it was legal to take his volunteer troops across the Rio Grande, he began preparing in earnest.[2]

His general plan was simple. First, he would cross the Rio Grande and occupy Matamoros; then he would move on to Monterrey, the capital of the state of Nuevo León, due west of Matamoros.[3] Considering the possibility of marching directly, he sent ahead a reconnaissance party under Captain Ben McCulloch. McCulloch reported back that the direct route lacked a sufficient water supply for Taylor's entire army, so Taylor was forced to take his army most of the way along the river and turn inland at Camargo. Part of his force would move to Camargo by water along the river; the other portion would march overland across the sandy wastes.

In one matter Taylor needed help: he needed to protect his incoming merchant ships and his supply base from Mexican naval action at Point Isabel. He also required boats to take a portion of his army up the Rio Grande. To those ends he requested a meeting with Commodore David Conner.

Taylor and Conner had never met before, and each was anxious to show the utmost courtesy to the other. Conner, knowing of Taylor's informal ways, came to the meeting in civilian clothes. Taylor, having heard of Conner's customary correctness in military matters, took his wrinkled dress uniform out of his trunk and for the only time in the war donned the uniform of his rank. After the two recovered from their surprise at this reversal, they got down to business.

Taylor was not disappointed. Conner was a punctilious man but the soul of cooperation, and he gave Taylor all the help he needed without permission from the Navy Department in Washington.

On May 17, the heavy mortars that Taylor had requested arrived, and Old Zack decided the time had come to cross over and seize Matamoros. At the same time, General Arista, still in command, sent a request for a truce. The two armies, Arista argued, could bide their time and allow the Mexican and American governments to settle their disputes politically. Taylor would have none of it. He demanded that Arista evacuate Matamoros, leaving all government property behind him. If Arista met that condition, Taylor promised that he would not pursue him inland. He demanded a reply within twelve hours. When the time was up with no word from Arista, Taylor made an assault crossing of the river, only to learn that the town had already been evacuated. Arista had taken all his guns with him but had left a few hundred wounded in the local hospitals.

Taylor immediately laid down an edict to govern Matamoros. He treated the townspeople generously, hoping to ensure that the people of Mexico regarded the Americans as friends. He encamped his army outside of the town and detailed only two companies of infantry to patrol the streets. For supplies, especially food, he paid the price the Mexican vendors asked, even if they sometimes overcharged him. He cared for the Mexican wounded and avoided any interference with the normal life of the city. Then, on August 4, he moved out for Camargo.

By this time, Taylor had received a contingent of general officers, newly appointed by President Polk and all of them Democrats. Fortunately, they were by and large good choices. The most promising was Major General William O. Butler of Kentucky, a veteran of the War of 1812. Another promising man was Brigadier General John Quitman of Mississippi, who had participated in the Black Hawk War. He already had two regular generals, David Twiggs, who had been promoted to regular brigadier general in Washington, and Brevet Brigadier General William Worth, who had returned with deep chagrin after having missed the battles of Palo Alto and Resaca de la Palma. There were also three other brigadiers.[4] If Taylor was to suffer any shortages in the coming campaign, the shortage would not be in generals. He wished, in fact, that he had not quite so many.

Taylor arrived in person at Camargo before the middle of August, having sent Worth's First Brigade ahead as an advance guard.[5] Twiggs soon followed with the Second Brigade. The volunteer units came to Camargo one at a time, being organized into Butler's "Field Division" when they arrived.

Taylor's army camped at Camargo for a little over a month, while he gathered supplies, mules, and guns. The camp was a strange mixture of tranquility and tragedy. It was vividly described by a witness, Captain Luther Giddings of the First Ohio Volunteers, who dropped in to call on General Taylor and found him dressed in a neat but comfortable linen suit, standing at the edge of his tent doing nothing but twirling his straw hat with his finger. After a short visit, Taylor asked Giddings to pay a similar call on General Worth, the official camp commander. Taylor was informal in personal appearance, but he adhered to the niceties of military protocol.

Giddings also took a somewhat surreptitious look at the camp of the regulars and was struck by its perfect order, in contrast with the confusion that reigned among the volunteers. Taylor actually commanded two armies, one regular and one volunteer, and the regulars, Giddings could see, were a privileged class.

This disparity between the regulars and volunteers carried more significance than mere show and spit and polish. It involved men's health, even their survival. Camargo was located three miles up the San Juan River from its junction with the Rio Grande, and it was a disastrous spot for a camp. The ground was so soft as to create a cesspool, and disease was rampant. During the time Taylor's army stayed there, a full one-eighth of his men died of disease, and nearly all those deaths came from the ranks of the volunteers because their camp lacked the discipline, cleanliness, and advantageous location of the regular camp. It was the enthusiastic, patriotic young Americans, who had left home in a burst of zeal, who were paying the price. Taylor regretted all this, but as a veteran of Fort Harrison thirty-two years earlier, he was not unduly upset at the prospect of losses to disease.

In the meantime, however, pressures back in the United States were growing for a move ahead toward Monterrey. By early August three months had passed since the public had received the heady news of Resaca de la Palma, and the American people, who knew nothing of Taylor's problems, were wondering why the reports of victories had ceased. Taylor was now being dubbed "General Delay." Word of this reached Taylor, and it only reinforced his desire to move southward out of the unhealthy conditions his army was enduring at Camargo. He calculated, however, that the paltry number of wagons and mules available would limit the force he took to only six thousand men. He therefore took all his three thousand regulars and three thousand volunteers.

Selecting which volunteer units to take with him and those he would have to leave behind—four thousand of them—was a difficult decision. Taylor based his selections on the physical condition of the various units. He also, as he reported back to Washington with apparent pride, tried to take with him representatives of as many states as possible.

For the forthcoming campaign, Taylor had organized his army into three divisions: the First Division was to be commanded by Twiggs, the Second Division by Worth, and the Volunteer Division (a whopping three thousand men) by William O. Butler. The first of these to set out for Cerralvo, sixty miles up the San Juan River, was Worth's, which left late in August. Worth was to be followed in a few days by Twiggs, and Butler was to bring up the rear. By now Taylor had attained the services of the Second Regiment of Texas Mounted Volunteers, known more familiarly as the Texas Rangers.

Taylor found the rangers were a mixed blessing. They were great fighters, but they did things their own way. Their commander, Colonel Jack Hays, refused to accompany Taylor on the march. A law unto himself, he advised that the rangers would take another route and meet Taylor's main body at some point of Hays's choice before they reached Monterrey. The rangers had an agenda that involved missions other than supporting Taylor. One was seeking their bitter enemy, Antonio Canales.

On the march, Taylor's troops generally fared as well as their individual unit discipline dictated. Some regiments made the march to Cerralvo easily; others barely survived. It was not long, however, before all of Taylor's men felt the exhilaration of the highlands of Nuevo León, out of the mud and heat of the Rio Grande Valley. The air was clear and cool, and the small, swift streams were clear and sparkling. Danger was minimal as far as Cerralvo, so Taylor sent his three divisions split up into smaller brigades; from then on they would be entering dangerous territory and would have to travel by whole divisions.

Taylor's next destination after Cerralvo was the small town of Marin, from where, in the clear air, an observer could make out the city of Monterrey, twenty-five miles in the distance. As the Army of Occupation approached Marin, Twiggs's First Division was in the lead. Its advance guard consisted of a company of the Washington-Baltimore Battalion, commanded by Captain John R. Kenly.[6]

On the morning of September 15, Kenly's advance guard reached a hill overlooking Marin. There he halted and crept up to the crest to survey the scene. The town, it appeared, was deserted. Just as he was preparing to move out, Kenly heard the sound of horses' hooves coming up behind him. He turned around and to his surprise the newcomer was Taylor himself, with only a couple of aides.

Taylor wasted no time in dismounting and walking over to greet an astonished Kenly. Extending his hand, Taylor mentioned their meeting a few weeks earlier at Matamoros. Then, after viewing the situation, he gave Kenly instructions. He was to approach the town cautiously, and if the enemy had vacated, he was to pass all the way through to the far edge and wait for the rest of the division to catch up with him. Taylor then rode off.

Kenly, complying with Taylor's orders, approached Marin and, finding it vacated, went through as directed. Off in the distance he spied Torrejon's cavalry lurking hesitatingly and then trotting slowly off. A freshly killed civilian lying in a doorway in town provided ample evidence that Torrejon had been there. But what impressed Kenly most about the episode was Taylor's amazing memory in remembering not only his name but also the circumstances of their meeting.

• • •

Marin was Taylor's last stop on the way to Monterrey, and all the men in his army prepared themselves mentally for the coming battle, which they knew would be bloody. Word had come in that Pedro de Ampudia, in command of the Mexican force in the north, had an army larger than Taylor's. The Americans expected him to fight desperately, knowing that this was his last chance for glory. President Antonio López de Santa Anna, recently returned from his exile in Cuba, would soon be taking the field himself. Taylor therefore assembled his whole army at Marin. Fortunately Jack Hays and his rangers appeared at Marin. It took until the morning of September 18, however, before the last of Butler's division marched in.

Based on what information was available, Old Zack had already formulated a tentative plan for attacking the city, which was, itself, a fortress. The stone buildings were flat topped, making perfect platforms for the defenders to fire down the straight streets. The key terrain feature, however, was not the town itself but Independence Hill, a long ridge running east-west. It was located on the west side of the town, and on its eastern tip stood the Bishop's Palace, which looked straight down on the city streets. Besides dominating Monterrey, Independence Hill stood on the north bank of the Santa Catarina River, Ampudia's supply line to Saltillo.

Since Taylor was coming in from the northeast, his problem was to reach Independence Hill without subjecting his army to flanking fire from the city. His problem was heightened by a grim fortress north of town, which was reportedly capable of holding four hundred soldiers and of mounting thirty guns. Though its proper name was the Citadel, the Americans respectfully referred to it as the Black Fort.

Ampudia's defense had one glaring defect: considerable distances lay between its various positions. Therefore, if Ampudia were to stay confined in his fortress without attacking outside—which Taylor expected—then the Americans could concentrate on reducing his strongpoints one at a time, for they could not support each other.

Taylor took a calculated risk. Assuming that Ampudia would remain passive, he split his forces. Worth's division, reinforced by the Texas Rangers and other troops, would leave Taylor's headquarters, which he called Walnut Grove, the day before the rest of the army and make a sweeping movement north of the Black Fort, cross the Santa Catarina River some distance to the west, and attack Independence Hill from the south. Once Worth had a foothold on the hill, he would turn east to take the Bishop's Palace, making Ampudia's position untenable. Meanwhile, Taylor, with the remainder of his army, would make a demonstration on the town east of the Black Fort to keep the Mexicans pinned down.

Operations at Monterrey officially went on for five days, from September 20 to September 24. The actual battle took only three days, from the twenty-first through the twenty-third. And unfortunately, if Resaca de la Palma had shown Taylor at his best, the first day at Monterrey showed him at his worst. His vague instructions allowed his aggressive subordinates to become embroiled, and what was intended as a mere demonstration became a major battle. As a result, both Twiggs's and Butler's divisions ended the day exhausted, their ranks partially depleted. They would be unfit for battle on the second day.

Meanwhile, Worth fared much better. Leaving Taylor on September 20, he had completed his flanking march around the Black Fort by the morning of September 21. Without delay he crossed the Santa Catarina, took the smaller Federation Hill to the south, recrossed the river to the north bank, and by the end of the day was in possession of the Bishop's Palace. On the twenty-third Taylor's wing was ready for a more coordinated attack on the east side of town, while Worth began his attack from the west.

No fighting occurred on September 24, and on the morning of the twenty-fifth Ampudia proposed a truce, much as had Arista at Matamoros. Ampudia agreed to evacuate the city of Monterrey and the Black Fort, in exchange for which Taylor would promise not to pursue him for a period of eight weeks, or until both sides heard from their respective governments. In that interim all hostilities would be suspended. Never mind that Taylor's superiors in Washington had forbidden him to accept a truce under any circumstances, his army was exhausted, disorganized, and in need of resupply. So after a certain amount of haggling between representatives of the two sides, Ampudia and his men marched out. The Americans marched into Monterrey with the bands playing "Yankee Doodle."

As they watched their foes leave, Taylor and his men realized that to be in possession of Monterrey at all was something to be thankful for. The brawny Mexican troops looked neither exhausted nor beaten. Ampudia himself may have been defeated, but these tough soldiers had not.

President Polk received Taylor's message describing events at Monterrey on Sunday, October 11, 1846. He was surprisingly angry at what should have been regarded as a cause for joy. Not only had Taylor's army achieved a significant victory but this turn of events, Polk expected, would induce the Mexican government to settle for a negotiated peace, conceding all the Mexican territory that Polk coveted.

Polk's bitterness toward Taylor's agreeing to an eight-week truce was less against the truce itself than his general's action in signing it against Polk's specific orders. The American public, however, was exultant with the news, so Polk was once more forced to show the public a happy face and even promote Taylor to the rank of major general in the regular army.

Accordingly, though Polk congratulated Taylor and his troops in public, he directed Secretary of War William Marcy to send off what was obviously a rebuke. For starters, the message expressed regret "that it was not deemed advisable to insist on the terms first proposed"—that is, surrender of Ampudia's army. Secondly, it instructed Taylor to "give the requisite notice that the armistice is to cease at once."

The message arrived at Taylor's camp outside Monterrey only four days before the truce was scheduled to expire. It therefore had no effect on the military situation. But it carried a consequence that Polk may have underestimated: it caused a drastic change in Zachary Taylor. In his rage, Taylor sent the messenger who had brought the dispatch on the rest of the way to give the notice to Ampudia himself.

7

Buena Vista

By early November 1846, American forces had accomplished everything that President Polk had thought necessary to induce the Mexican government to make territorial settlements based on Polk's terms. Brigadier General Stephen W. Kearny had taken Santa Fe, Zachary Taylor had taken Monterrey, and Polk expected word any day that California was safely in American hands. A reasonable Mexican government, Polk believed, would see the futility of continuing the war and meet his terms. But the president was ignorant of the situation in Mexico City—that Mexican president Santa Anna could never stay in power if he performed an act so shameful in Mexican eyes. The war would drag on.

Polk, however, saw time as being on his side, and he came up with a plan he termed "masterful inaction." American forces would merely occupy the territories they had taken, which included all that he had sought and more. Let the Mexicans make the next move. Inevitably, sooner or later, Santa Anna or his successor would have to agree to a negotiated peace.

Polk and his cabinet were satisfied with this plan, and they considered the matter settled. So when Senator Thomas Hart Benton returned from Missouri for the opening of the Thirtieth Congress, Polk expected him to approve. Benton, who had opposed the war, was now reconciled to it, and Polk looked upon him as a trusted adviser. To Polk's surprise, however, Benton protested. "Masterful inaction" was not his style, he said. The United States should send an overpowering force to land at the Mexican port of Veracruz and march inland and occupy Mexico City. Only when faced with such a stark turn of events would the Mexicans capitulate. Polk, surprisingly, agreed on the spot. He may have secretly harbored doubts about masterful inaction anyway.

That question settled, the discussion then turned to a more difficult subject: who would command the proposed expedition? None of the regular army generals would be fit, for political reasons. Polk wanted a good Democrat to reap the glories of military victory. He therefore tried to persuade Congress to create the new grade of lieutenant general, who would automatically become the head of the army. Benton agreed and without undue hesitation volunteered that he himself would be just the man to assume that position.

Polk concurred in that outlandish scheme, but the Congress did not. So eventually Polk concluded, much to his regret, that by default Scott would have to lead the forthcoming invasion. The general-in-chief was so grateful that he nearly broke down in tears, and before Polk could change his mind, Scott departed Washington for New York, where he awaited a ship to take him to the Brazos.

At this point Scott and Taylor were on cordial terms, and Scott was concerned for Taylor's feelings about being replaced, or at least overshadowed. While in New York, Scott wrote Taylor giving hints but no details of plans afoot. He tried to assuage Taylor's inevitable disappointment with compliments. Scott's letter, however, sounded pompous and patronizing:

> I am not coming, my dear general, to supersede you in the immediate command on the line of operations rendered illustrious by you and your gallant army. My proposed theater is different.
>
> But, my dear general, I shall be obliged to take from you most of the gallant officers and men (regulars and volunteers) whom you have so long and nobly commanded. . . .

But I rely on your patriotism to submit to the temporary sacrifice with cheerfulness. No man can better afford to do so.

Taylor, in the meantime, had assumed that masterful inaction was the right tactic and was busy deploying his forces for an extended occupation of northern Mexico. He began occupying key places at about the time that Polk had been conferring with Benton. With Commodore Conner occupying Tampico, Taylor was planning to send troops to reinforce him. He also intended to occupy Saltillo. He would thus be holding the line, west to east, of Saltillo, Monterrey, and Tampico.

On November 8, 1846, Taylor received welcome news and unwelcome news. He was elated to receive a message advising that Brigadier General John E. Wool, with thirteen hundred men, had arrived at Monclava, a town about one hundred miles northwest of Monterrey. Wool's original mission had called for him to move westward from San Antonio to join with Colonel Alexander Doniphan's Missouri volunteers at Chihuahua. When scouts had reported that the route to Chihuahua lacked water, Wool decided to place himself under Taylor's command, and he recommended to Taylor that Wool should continue on to Parras, where he would cut a main road to San Luis Potosí. Taylor agreed. Parras was not far from Saltillo, and he was glad for the reinforcement. On the same day as he received Wool's message, Taylor ordered Worth to march his Second Division to Saltillo, sixty miles to the southwest.

Then came the bad news: a message arrived from Secretary of War Marcy giving a "suggestion" that Taylor make no further moves inland—that is, to Saltillo—and to protect his army he should concentrate his troops at Monterrey. Marcy's suggestion was based on something Taylor did not know: he would soon lose the bulk of his force.

Taylor was angry and in that state of mind decided to ignore Marcy's message and go ahead with his original plans. Marcy's message had, after all, been couched in the form of a "suggestion," and though a "suggestion" from a superior is usually considered to be an order, the term afforded Taylor the latitude to rationalize rejecting it. In mid-December, he left Monterrey with Twiggs's division, which he was sending to Tampico. He planned to accompany Twiggs about halfway.

Scott arrived at the Brazos at Christmastime, and he determined to make a trip up the Rio Grande to Camargo to meet with Taylor in person to discuss troop deployment and future tactics. Though he issued Taylor no orders to return from Monterrey to greet him at Camargo, he naturally expected him to do so. But on Scott's arrival at Camargo he found Taylor absent. Though Taylor later claimed to be unaware of Scott's plans, his excuse was unconvincing.

With or without Taylor, Scott had to take action immediately. The Veracruz expedition was to be the main thrust of the war, and to execute it he needed the best troops available, which meant Taylor's two divisions of regulars and Butler's Field Division. He therefore acted on his own; he took the troops he needed and left a letter for Taylor explaining what he had done. He was taking, he said,

Two regiments of regular dragoons
All of Taylor's voluntary cavalry
Two batteries of light field artillery
Twiggs' and Worth's divisions (4,000 men)
Butler's Volunteer (Field) Division (4,000 men)[1]

On receiving Scott's letter Taylor was furious, even though reassured that replacement units would soon report to him. Neither he nor Scott, however, was concerned about the immediate safety of his army, even though they knew that Santa Anna was assembling an army at San Luis Potosí, about two hundred miles south of Saltillo. Between the two cities lay a large desert, along which all water tanks had recently been destroyed. That desert, they reasoned, would discourage Santa Anna from moving north.

The Americans, however, were unaware of events currently transpiring in Mexico City. They did not realize how much Santa

Anna needed a victory of some kind to bolster his personal popularity with the Mexican people. They were also unaware that he had a copy of Scott's recent letter to Taylor telling about a planned amphibious operation, presumably against Veracruz. Based on that information, Santa Anna calculated that such an operation could not be launched immediately. In the meantime he could move north with a strong force and destroy Taylor before needing to turn his attention to the larger expedition. He had amassed a fairly well-trained and well-equipped army, which he intended to lead personally to Saltillo. By late January 1847, he had been afforded a full four months to train and equip them.

The lead division of Santa Anna's army left San Luis Potosí on January 28, to be followed by another division each day, a force of twenty thousand in all. It soon became apparent that the Mexican dictator had underestimated the difficulties. After thirty miles, his army reached the desert, where at first it encountered freezing rain so severe that some men died of cold. Ten days later the weather en route became broiling hot. With the water tanks destroyed and no water available, discipline broke down. As a result, Santa Anna lost a quarter of his strength in less than three weeks. The strongest of his troops, however, survived; Santa Anna had the temerity to hold a lavish review of his army and basked in the *vivas* of his men.

• • •

In the meantime, Taylor was receiving new volunteer troops every day to replace the veterans that Scott had taken. His total, however, fell well short of his expectations. Though new regiments were arriving every day, he still could not occupy all the key points in the region, and for security's sake he ordered all the scattered troops to concentrate at Saltillo. Except for artillery and some cavalry, his new army was almost all volunteer. It consisted of eight infantry regiments, among which, much to Taylor's pleasure, was the Mississippi Rifles, commanded by his onetime son-in-law and new-found ally, Jefferson Davis. The total strength of the army, including the sick, came to fewer than five thousand men. Still Taylor had confidence that he could defeat the Mexicans, even at an advanced location south of Saltillo.

By February 21, Taylor had marched through Saltillo and concentrated his army at Agua Nueva, some eighteen miles south of the city. By now he knew that a fight was imminent, so he sent out a force of dragoons under Colonel Charles May, of Resaca fame, who reported encountering Santa Anna's army within an easy day's march of Taylor's position. Still Old Zack made no move until later in the day, when Ben McCulloch of the Texas Rangers reported Santa Anna to be even closer, only six miles away. It was time to get ready to fight.

Taylor intended to make a stand at Agua Nueva, despite the fact that his flanks were open, the ground was flat, and he was vastly outnumbered. He was challenged, however, by General John Wool, who had joined him from nearby Parras. The position was too exposed, Wool insisted, strongly recommending that the army fall back a few miles to a spot just south of the Hacienda de Buena Vista.

Taylor bristled; he had never retreated from an enemy before, he growled, and did not intend to start now. Wool, however, persisted, so Taylor, who had great respect for Wool and probably realized that he was right, placed Wool in temporary command with orders to drop back and organize a defensive position at a place called the Narrows, a few miles south of Buena Vista. He personally would ride back and check on the security of his supply depot at Saltillo, much as he had done at Point Isabel nine months earlier. He returned to the new position the next morning, February 22.

The defensive position that Wool had established at the Narrows was strong, and it was only by the most incredible luck that such a piece of terrain could be found in the vicinity. The key to its strength lay in the fact that the main road between San Luis Potosí and Saltillo ran through a defile, protected on the west by a set of impassable gullies, enabling him to concentrate his army on the east. The only approach from that direction was along a flat ridge called the Plateau by the Americans. The fortunate thing about the

Plateau was that it could not be scaled except at a point more than a mile away. It was ideal for Taylor's flying artillery, since it was devoid of cover and concealment: it would comprise a superb killing ground.

Wool had placed three of Captain John Washington's six artillery pieces on the San Luis Potosí–Saltillo road, prepared to fire southward, protected by two infantry regiments atop the west end of the Plateau and a few troops in the gullies across the road just in case. At the far end of the Plateau, Wool placed three infantry regiments, each reinforced with two or three guns from Washington's, Bragg's, and Sherman's artillery batteries.

A weakness of the American position was that it could be bypassed by an enemy making a wide sweep around the left flank. That route could not be used, however, until Santa Anna eliminated the American infantry units guarding its east approach. From the end of the Plateau on the east the ground rose abruptly, making a sharp hill (Sierra). The slopes of the Sierra were rough, however, and it led not to the Narrows position but to Saltillo in the American rear. Should the enemy try to bypass his position along that route, Wool reasoned, there would be sufficient warning. He therefore placed no troops up on the mountain in his first deployment.

• • •

On the Mexican side, Santa Anna's plan was a good one, if conventional. Recognizing the strength of the American position at the Narrows, he sent only one of his four divisions up the Saltillo road toward Washington's guns as a diversion. His main effort consisted of two divisions that he sent around to the far end of the Plateau to outflank the Narrows from the east. He held his fourth division in reserve. He sent some of Ampudia's troops up on the Sierra, with some cavalry, but they did not push on, probably for fear of being cut off from the rear.

Taylor arrived on the field at 11:00 AM on February 22 to the loud cheers of his troops. Wool was a competent military craftsman, but Taylor was their hero, and they would brook nobody else to command them. On his arrival, Old Zack received a pompous message from Santa Anna, asserting that Taylor was now faced with a mighty twenty-thousand-man army—never mind the facts—and that Taylor's destruction was inevitable. Santa Anna promised that if Taylor surrendered, he and his men would receive treatment "with the consideration belonging to the Mexican character." Taylor is reported to have received this message with a bit of profanity, but he answered merely,

> In reply to your note of this date, summoning me to surrender my forces at your direction, I beg leave to say that I decline acceding to your request.

Taylor's defiant message may have lacked the drama of General Anthony McAuliffe's "Nuts" at Bastogne a century later,[2] but it conveyed the message.

The battle began that afternoon, but it consisted only of a repulse of the division on the Saltillo road and a fight between a Mexican division and a couple of Taylor's cavalry regiments up on the Sierra. The American cavalry eventually withdrew down to the base but still in a position protecting the Plateau. Anticipating no further action, Taylor, always concerned about the vulnerability of his rear, returned that night to Saltillo, taking Davis's Mississippi Rifles as escort. He returned to his position at the Narrows the next morning.

He returned none too soon. After a miserable night in the cold, the two armies had begun to fight in earnest early in the day. At the Narrows, Washington's artillery battery had experienced no difficulty in again repulsing the Mexican division, but up at the head of the Plateau, Santa Anna's two enveloping divisions had temporarily routed the two regiments of Indiana and Illinois volunteers that Wool had placed there. To Taylor's surprise, Wool was dispirited. "General," he said, "we are whipped."

Taylor was unusually sharp. "That is for me to determine," he snapped. He then sent the Mississippi Rifles forward to stem the flow of retreating Americans—which it did—and then settled into his customary position for directing a battle, sidesaddle on Old Whitey, chawing on a plug of tobacco.

The situation, as Taylor saw it, was serious but far from hopeless. On the minus side, Santa Anna had destroyed three of Taylor's volunteer regiments: the Arkansas and Kentucky cavalry regiments and the Second Indiana Infantry, thus weakening Taylor's army considerably. But though Santa Anna had gained a foothold on the Plateau, he had failed to take any terrain that Taylor considered critical.

Santa Anna then tried a new scheme: he contained the Americans on the Plateau while he sent his reserve division down the next ridge to the right, farther in Taylor's rear. Taylor quickly detected what was afoot. He sent the overworked Mississippians and the newly arrived Third Indiana Infantry, reinforced with Bragg's artillery battery, to stem the advance. Together the two regiments were drawn up before the Mexicans arrived. They assumed an odd formation. Instead of making a straight line, they formed up at an angle, creating the famous "inverted V." They waited until the Mexicans came within seventy-five yards of their positions before letting go with simultaneous fire all at once, infantry and artillery together. The Mexican division crumbled. The Americans closed in for the kill but were interrupted by a sudden thunderstorm and a ruse in the form of an offer to parley, which delayed action and allowed many of the intended victims to escape.

That attack provided grist for the mill of Taylor's reputation as a cool, imperturbable commander. He was later depicted as standing behind Bragg saying calmly, "A little more grape, Captain Bragg."

Taylor then committed his worst mistake of the battle: he attacked on the Plateau. His volunteers had performed beyond all expectations in defensive actions, but the attack called for better-trained troops. Overestimating the extent of his temporary advantage, he sent six companies of the First Illinois to pursue the retreating Mexicans. The Mexicans, seeing the small size of the force, halted their retreat and closed in on the small force of Americans. Two other American regiments, seeing the plight of the men from Illinois, joined in the battle. This was not the kind of fighting that Taylor's army could endure. With the Mexican advantage in strength, he could ill afford a battle of attrition. Fortunately, Taylor was able to bring all three of his artillery batteries into play and the survivors were rescued. Both sides pulled back after indecisive action.

The Army of Occupation had held the field of Buena Vista against vastly superior numbers but it was still in grave danger. In a day and a half's fighting Taylor had lost 673 officers and men killed and wounded, and an incredible number, 1,500, to desertion.[3] His men were exhausted and supplies were alarmingly low. As soon as the day's fighting was over, Taylor rode back again to Saltillo, this time to seek resupply and reinforcements. Again he took the Mississippi Rifles with him but this time to leave them there for a rest. Their commander, Jefferson Davis, had been wounded in the ankle and could no longer command in person.

At Saltillo, Taylor received great news. Two new infantry regiments had arrived and more were expected to arrive soon. Perhaps more significant was the arrival of fifty supply wagons. Taylor's army was now as strong as it had been before the beginning of the battle.

On the morning of February 24, Taylor returned early to the Narrows. As dawn arose, he and John Wool stood together to try to make out what Santa Anna was up to. As it became light, the Americans could perceive that, whereas thousands of brightly colored Mexican uniforms had been visible the day before, there were now only a few Mexicans, tending the overnight fires. Santa Anna had left the field. Taylor's army was safe. He and Wool embraced each other in joy.

• • •

Santa Anna had apparently made his decision for quitting the field based on the exhaustion of both his supplies and his troops. The explanation he offered to the people of Mexico, however, was that the degenerating political situation in Mexico City called for his immediate return. Besides, he could boast that he had "stopped" Taylor in the latter's supposed drive to Mexico City. Santa Anna had captured enough American regimental colors to give credence to his claim.

Santa Anna's posturing, however, was of little interest to Zachary Taylor. He moved his army down the road to Agua Nueva, where he penned a triumphant message back to Washington: "No result so decisive could have been obtained by holding Monterrey." After a short passage of time, however, he evacuated Agua Nueva and even Saltillo and concentrated back at Monterrey.

Buena Vista had been a costly victory. Among the dead from this unnecessary battle were many fine Americans, among whom were at least two prominent political figures. Colonel Archibald Yell of the Arkansas Cavalry had been governor of his home state. Lieutenant Colonel Henry Clay Jr. of the Kentucky volunteers was also killed. It seems particularly ironic that Clay was the son of the man whose political ambitions had virtually been ended in 1844 by his opposition to picking a quarrel with Mexico.

The Buena Vista campaign was fraught with ironies that proved to be of political consequence. Taylor's very presence in that exposed position was a blunder, brought on, or at least encouraged, by his resentment of Polk and Scott and their supposed plotting against him. And yet that very blunder—or perhaps the public perception of Taylor as David being sent unnecessarily to face the Goliath Santa Anna—was the factor that elevated a potentially strong political candidate to a virtually unbeatable one.

8

The Election of 1848

The exact point at which Zachary Taylor made a final decision to run for the office of president of the United States is a matter of conjecture. The decision was a big one, for in so doing he was laying his reputation on the line to enter a field in which he was a newcomer. A general knows the men he is working with, some of them very well and a few of them intimately. But when he enters the political arena, he is likely to know few of his future associates, even fewer of them intimately.

There have been, of course, some military men whose egos were such that they contemplated running for the presidency even before achieving the victories that made a political career realistic. Douglas MacArthur and Winfield Scott come to mind in that category.[1] But it is also noteworthy that neither of these men attained his goal, although Scott was nominated by the Whigs in 1852, only to be trounced in the general election.

Though Taylor held strong resentments against both Polk and Scott, his animosity did not at first mean that he was developing any political ambitions. In a letter written in late January 1847, he expressed concern only for his own military reputation and the campaign ahead. The letter denied any political aspirations and gives every impression of being sincere. Later, just before the Battle of Buena Vista, he wrote,

On the subject of the Presidency, I am free to say, under no circumstances have I any aspirations for the office nor do I have
the vanity to consider myself qualified for the station. . . . [2]

Taylor had every reason to be reticent about politics. Generals,
even those uniformly successful up to the moment, do not dare
think of anything, including politics, until they are sure that they
have won their last battle. In addition, Taylor's letters were written
before the aura of the victory at Buena Vista transformed a military hero into a political contender.

• • •

Kentucky senator John Crittenden was the man with whom Taylor
did most of his corresponding. He was one of the most colorful
and influential politicians of the mid-nineteenth century. Born in
1787, he was almost Taylor's age and, like Taylor, served in the War
of 1812 as a major. Except when in Washington, Crittenden lived
all his life in Frankfort, Kentucky. In the Senate, he was courted by
politicians of all stripes, but especially by the Whigs. In person he
was of moderate height, slight of build, with a full head of gray
hair and a facial expression which in repose seemed dour, becloud-
ing the genial nature that lay underneath.

Crittenden first entered the Senate in 1819, at age thirty-two,
but he stayed only a short time. He could not, he claimed, afford to
raise his large family on a senator's pay, and he immediately resigned. He spent the next sixteen years in Frankfort practicing law
and serving in local positions. Then, having amassed enough of an
estate to be able to survive on a paltry governmental salary, he returned to the Senate in 1835 and remained there until 1848, when
he was drafted by the Whigs to run for governor of Kentucky. He
was engaged in that campaign at the same time that Taylor was
running for president.

Crittenden was always regarded as a kingmaker. A whiskey-
drinking, gambling man, he was also a shrewd politician. His reputation for discretion and loyalty won him many friends, who knew

that they could express themselves freely to him without fear of his violating their confidences. He put that reputation to good avail politically, because as the staunchest of Whigs he was able to form political judgments based on an intimate knowledge of the political participants.

Crittenden was also a realist, keenly aware that the Whigs had always been a minority party. He regarded their dismal electoral record with a cold eye. As of 1848, he was aware, the party had won only one presidential election since its founding in 1834 as a protest against the policies of Andrew Jackson. And in that single victory, which had come in 1840, their candidate, Senator William Henry Harrison, had marched under the banner of his questionable military victory at Tippecanoe nearly thirty years earlier. In planning for 1848, therefore, Crittenden forsook the man he had consistently supported, his fellow Kentuckian Henry Clay. He began looking at both Winfield Scott and Zachary Taylor as possible candidates from the moment the Mexican War erupted in early 1846.

Both Scott and Taylor had responded with enthusiasm to the proffered friendship of the Kentucky senator. Both developed the habit of baring their feelings to him by letter, nearly always at least including some protests against real or supposed slights at the hands of the Democratic administration of James Polk. Scott wrote far more often than Taylor, and sometimes his missives were so full of self-pity that Crittenden must have found him a bore.

In early 1846, however, Crittenden's problem of choosing between the two military heroes appeared to be solved. Scott's worst enemy had always been his pen, and once war had broken out, he sought to replace Taylor in the field by writing letters, not only to Crittenden but also to Secretary of War William Marcy, who was no friend. Marcy happily aired a couple of his letters, and the public found Scott's self-pitying tone a subject for ridicule. For the time being, Scott's political prospects appeared dead. Crittenden thus became Taylor's supporter, even in the days before Taylor developed any desire for that support.

•   •   •

Political chaos is not uncommon in a free society, and the year 1848 was more chaotic than most because of the virulence of the growing disagreement over the prospect of the expansion of slavery into the territories gained by force from Mexico and by negotiation with Britain. For years, ever since the Missouri Compromise of 1820, the issue of slavery had lain relatively quiet on the national scene, though always bubbling beneath the surface on the local level. By 1848 Texas's annexation to the Union had threatened to upset the balance between slave and free states, especially in the United States Senate. But the controversy extended far beyond Texas alone. The question of the disposition of the new territories of California, New Mexico, and Utah was equally important. Should they come into the Union as slave or free if and when admitted?

The two major political parties had avoided taking sides on the issue. In general, northern Democrats were less hostile to slavery than northern Whigs. In the border South, where the Whigs were strong, they tended to be less supportive of slavery than Democrats. The same attitude, though more pronounced, prevailed in the Deep South.

As a result of these shades of intensity, the voting in the 1844 presidential election had been checkered. States in the North could go Democratic and southern states could go Whig. For example, Andrew Jackson's Democratic stronghold Tennessee had gone Whig, even though the Democratic nominee, James K. Polk, was from Tennessee. But in 1848, both parties, or portions thereof, saw a military hero as a potential winner. The situation even before Monterrey has been described thus by Taylor's biographer Holman Hamilton.

> Taylor's admirers in 1846 and 1847 were an odd assortment of political allies. Whigs predominated on his bandwagon, but almost every party was represented. There were Northern

Whigs like Abraham Lincoln, Southern Democrats like Jefferson Davis, Southern Whigs like Alexander H. Stephens, Northern Democrats like Simon Cameron, and Native Americans like Lewis C. Levin. . . . Spoils-hungry Whigs, looking for a winner; dissonant Democrats on the outs with Polk; Calhounites, looking for a Southerner in the White House— all eyed Zachary Taylor with interest.[3]

There were numerous other potential candidates, of course, but only three were to be taken seriously. One was Henry Clay, who still, despite his advanced age of seventy-one and the fact that he had been defeated in presidential bids three times, still seemed to harbor some hope.[4] That ambition caused Crittenden some embarrassment when he felt obliged to tell Clay of his own transfer of support to Taylor.

The second candidate was Winfield Scott, general-in-chief of the army. Scott's victories in Mexico had by now erased his earlier follies in the public mind, but President Polk scuttled his ambitions by ordering him to face a court of inquiry as to the conduct of the recent campaign in Mexico. Though the court totally approved of Scott's handling of the war, the proceeding had taken so much time that Scott was seriously handicapped in organizing for a presidential race. Besides, Taylor was a more appealing candidate. Better to carry a nickname of "Old Rough and Ready" than "Old Fuss and Feathers."

Not all Whigs were favorable to Taylor, of course. Many Northern antislavery men could not abide the thought of a slaveholder in the White House. Foremost among them was Horace Greeley, the influential editor of the *New York Tribune*. These militants, however, were shouted down by the bulk of the northern Whigs, who, while averse to slavery, were more realistic. These men saw in Taylor a moderate—a moderate who could be elected.

The most prominent of these Taylor supporters was Thurlow Weed, the undisputed Whig boss of New York State. Weed was second only to Crittenden as a Taylor asset, except for one thing: he was fickle. He occasionally leaned toward Senator John M. Clayton of Delaware, a man ten years younger than Taylor and a brilliant orator. Another possible candidate was Crittenden himself, though the senator immediately turned the prospect down. Crittenden was doubtless sincere in his refusal, but Clayton was questionable. His disadvantage was that he came from a small state. It is possible that his greatest significance in the election of 1848 lay in tempting the roving eye of Thurlow Weed.

• • •

For eight months following the Battle of Buena Vista, Taylor remained at Monterrey, where his presence with the Army of Occupation was important. We know today that Santa Anna's defeat at Buena Vista put a permanent end to any further plans to move north by the overland route, but the Mexican president did not say so in public. The possibility of another overland invasion from central Mexico was not to be discounted. By November 1847, however, after Scott had occupied Mexico City for two months, Taylor felt free to return home.

During that period Taylor's political support waned for a while. A contributing factor to the cooling off was the series of headlines reporting Scott's victories in his drive from Veracruz inland to Mexico City. For sheer military brilliance, it must be admitted, Scott's victories at Cerro Gordo, Contreras, and Mexico City far overshadowed those of Taylor.

A more important threat to Taylor's presidential prospects, however, was the attitude of Taylor himself. With time on his hands in Monterrey, he amused himself by writing to friends, and his letters did nothing to further his cause. Besides his constant railings against the Polk administration (which probably did him no harm politically), he constantly disavowed any interest in running for president. He would cheerfully support Henry Clay if Clay decided to run again, he insisted, though notably he usually added a caveat: that he would do so only if Clay were electable. At the same time, Taylor consistently refused to identify himself as a Whig.

Taylor's reluctance to commit himself is understandable. It is only natural for a military man to think of the electorate as he did of his soldiers, people who deserve equal consideration regardless of the political party they belong to. And Taylor had not, after all, worked up to his position of prominence through the ranks of the Whigs. But the effect of his frank and open views, spread through his correspondence, was to discourage those who did not know him. Partisan Whigs demanded assurance that, if elected, Taylor would follow the principles of the party. As William Seward of New York remarked to Thurlow Weed, what Taylor was writing from Monterrey would have ruined any other candidate.[5]

· · ·

When Taylor returned home, he learned firsthand what a national idol he had become. His world had completely changed. As described by Holman Hamilton,

> The soldier, who had won few honors in four decades on active duty, became the recipient of honors galore. Medals of bronze, silver and gold—swords, scabbards, sashes, medallions—were showered on him by grateful compatriots. Popular songs were dedicated to him. Girls strewed flowers in his path. Even more than his victories, the unassuming manner of Zachary Taylor endeared him to American civilians, while enshrining him in his comrades' hearts. And suddenly the warrior who never voted became the masses' favorite candidate for the highest office in the land.[6]

Taylor did not pause long in New Orleans to savor his newfound fame. He proceeded immediately to his plantation at Cypress Grove, near Baton Rouge. Here he could rest, enjoy reunions with his family, and inspect the various plantations he owned. It was a happy time because the overseers who ran his various properties had done well. His wife, Margaret, having been abandoned for so long, was grateful to have him back. She was, however, likely to be something of a burden politically. She devoutly desired domestic peace and quiet and constantly prayed that someone else, not Zack, would be nominated for the presidency. Meanwhile, Taylor continued to write letters refusing to identify himself as a Whig. As a result, the doubts haunting Thurlow Weed and others were becoming acute. The concern was shared by Taylor's entourage at Baton Rouge and New Orleans. The situation could not go on without something being done.

On April 22, 1848, a boat sailed up the Mississippi River from New Orleans and docked at Cypress Grove. It carried Taylor's aide Colonel William W. S. Bliss, who, though a regular army officer, had become a full-scale participant in Taylor's political life. Bliss had been in New York conferring with Weed. The word he brought was urgent: Taylor must declare himself a Whig.

By coincidence, the boat that brought Bliss to the landing below Taylor's home was also scheduled to take aboard three gentlemen who had been visiting Taylor. On meeting them on the dock, Bliss learned that the trio, Crittenden's southern lieutenants, had already accomplished what he had come to do; they had induced Taylor to declare himself a Whig.

Logan Hunton, James Love, and Bailey Peyton had not found Old Rough and Ready easy to deal with. Fortunately, they were persistent. They had decided on visiting Taylor some three days earlier while conferring in a New Orleans hotel. With the concurrence of other Taylor supporters, they had decided that a trip to Baton Rouge was necessary. Love, Hunton, and Peyton, accordingly, decided to go. Hunton, the driving spirit, drew up a draft of the letter they hoped Taylor would sign. The others approved the draft.

The three had arrived at Baton Rouge on Friday morning, April 21. Taylor personally met them at the dock, took them to his plantation, and showed them to their quarters. After dinner, Hunton read his draft letter, and Taylor made periodic comments—which Love dutifully jotted down. After dinner Love and Taylor met, and Love assured his host that all he had to do was sign a letter based

on the remarks he had made while Hunton had been reading his
own draft. Taylor reluctantly agreed to sign a letter including what
he had said that evening but no more.

That was enough. Love and Hunton retired to their rooms, and
Hunton worked late into the night composing a letter based on
Taylor's remarks. Taylor approved the message at breakfast the next
morning. The visitors then pushed their luck; they insisted that
Taylor copy the letter in his own handwriting. He addressed the
letter to Captain J. S. Allison of New Orleans, a close friend and the
widower of Taylor's late sister. Allison had little interest in the letter's contents, but he was a convenient addressee. The letter was
described as short, but only by the standards of the day; it went on
for pages and pages. But Taylor was accustomed to writing long letters; he had been doing so for months, and he acceded. Its critical
paragraphs were just what his visitors wanted.

I reiterate what I have often said . . . I am a Whig but not an
ultra Whig. If elected I would not be the mere president of a
party—I would endeavor to act independent of party domi-
nation and should feel bound to administer the Government
untrammelled by party schemes.

Second—the veto power—the power given by the Constitution to the Executive to exercise his veto is a high conser-
vative power; but in my opinion it should never be exercised
except in cases of clear violation of the Constitution, or man-
ifest haste or want of due consideration by the Congress—
Indeed I have thought for many years past, that known
opinions and wishes of the Executive have exercised undue
and injurious influence upon the Legislative Department of
the government and from this cause I have thought that our
system was in danger of undergoing a great change from its
true theory.

Hunton and Love were totally satisfied. They took Taylor's letter
with them and, as mentioned, showed it to Bliss when they met

him on the dock. Weed, Crittenden, and other Taylor supporters now had a concrete commitment with which they could work. The Whig nomination, they believed, was ensured.[7]

The First Allison Letter, as it came to be called, actually had less effect on Taylor's situation than might have been imagined. Certainly it had no effect on his determination to be his own man in the White House, and no great immediate swing in public opinion seemed to result from it. As the Whig convention neared, however, he was definitely the front-runner.

Taylor had protested against holding a Whig convention, even though national party conventions had become the norm from 1832 on. Holding such a spectacle would, in his opinion, emphasize his Whiggery, something he desired to avoid in order to maintain his broader appeal among voters of all party persuasions. Like Crittenden, he was well aware that the Whigs were still much in the minority.

Taylor's wishes regarding a convention were not, however, to be respected. He may have been the leading candidate for president, but he exercised no control over the Whig party machinery. Accordingly, the Whig delegates descended on Philadelphia in early June 1848 and opened their proceedings in the Chinese Museum on Ninth Street. Taylor, as was considered proper, remained at Cypress Grove, completely out of touch with what was going on.

John Crittenden proved his loyalty. Though running for governor of Kentucky, he took the time to act as Taylor's floor manager. Always sensitive to the feelings of those Whigs who were hostile to his candidate and hoping to attract independent voters, Crittenden avoided high-handed action to keep the goodwill of those states that had sent favorite sons, for example. So, even though he believed Taylor could be nominated on the first ballot, he let things ride, always confident of the ultimate outcome.

The convention got off with an unruly start, due to inadequate security measures to keep boisterous political enemies out of the hall. And then a Scott delegate got up and introduced a rule demanding that the nominee must agree to follow the decisions of the convention and to promote the Whig Party. The chairman, John M. Morehead of North Carolina, overruled the proposal as out of order. Then the names of the various nominees were introduced—Clay, Scott, Webster, Clayton, and Taylor.

On the first ballot, Taylor received a plurality but far from a majority: Taylor 111; Clay 98; Scott 43; and Webster 22. On the second ballot, Taylor picked up 7 delegates; Clay slipped to 86; Scott rose to 49; and Webster fell to 12. The trend continued until the fourth ballot on which Taylor garnered 171 votes; Scott 60; Clay 35; and Webster 17. Taylor now had a majority and became the party nominee.[8]

But not universally approved. Some of the northern delegates refused to join in the customary ritual of casting one extra ballot to make the vote unanimous. One delegate from Massachusetts rose to his feet and accused the convention of nominating a man who would "continue the rule of slavery for four more years," even proposing to declare the convention "dissolved." Though others voiced somewhat the same sentiments, most of the delegates were anxious to get on with the next order of business, the nomination of a vice president. Even Horace Greeley, despondent as he was, refrained from voicing a protest on the floor.[9]

The nomination for vice president was wide open, and the candidates were plentiful. Not all were willing. Names such as Thurlow Weed, who had no interest in the position, were brought up—even William Seward. The voting, however, was not long drawn out, because one man stood out above the rest, Millard Fillmore of New York. Granted, the name of Millard Fillmore does not figure prominently in our history books, but he was, except for Henry Clay, the most experienced Whig under consideration at the convention. He had been in contention for the vice presidency for several years and was said to have been disappointed when he was not nominated with Clay in 1844. There was little protest when Fillmore was chosen for the second spot.

. . .

Taylor, at Cypress Grove, seemed to show little interest in the drama being played out in Philadelphia. He was still a major general in the regular army and the owner of plantations to be overseen. His official position was commander of the Western Command, in charge of all army troops west of the Mississippi. His dual role as army officer and candidate was facilitated by the practice of the time that defined the headquarters of a command as being merely where the commander was—no need for large establishments with extensive staffs and communications. Taylor simply set up a headquarters a few miles away from Cypress Grove, staffed it with a couple of aides and presumably clerks, and kept his own schedule.[10]

The official notification of Taylor's nomination for president by the Whigs, in the form of a letter from John M. Morehead, presiding officer of the convention, arrived at the Baton Rouge post office on June 18, 1848. To everyone's surprise, Taylor did not reply for nearly a month. When he did so, he seemed unapologetic. He gracefully expressed his gratitude for the honor, though many considered his response too bland. The main interest on most people's part was Taylor's long delay. Did he really plan to accept the nomination? The Whigs had a right to wonder.

The delay turned out to be due to a misunderstanding between Taylor and the Baton Rouge postmaster. Taylor had notified the official that he would no longer pay for letters on which postage was due, and the official had thrown the Morehead letter into the dead-letter file.[11]

. . .

The Democrats had held their convention at Baltimore in late May, before the Whigs. Like the Whigs, their convention was open; President James K. Polk was upholding his pledge, made during the 1844 election, not to run for a second term. The slate the Democrats came up with was a pair of responsible, if perhaps colorless, candidates. Though neither carried the appeal of Zachary Taylor, they made a good team.

The presidential candidate, Lewis Cass of Michigan, was two years Taylor's senior in age, having been born in Exeter, New Hampshire, in 1782. He was very much a product of the eastern establishment, having attended Phillips Exeter Academy in the same town. He had participated in the War of 1812 as a brigadier general and was later appointed by President James Madison as governor of the Michigan Territory, a post he held for eighteen years. During that time, he had led an exploring expedition to find the headwaters of the Mississippi River, since that location was deemed of some importance in the continuing negotiations between the United States and Britain over the boundary between the United States and Canada.

In 1831, Cass resigned his post in Michigan to serve as secretary of war under President Andrew Jackson. During his tenure, he was credited with—or accused of—playing a major role in Jackson's policy of removing all the Indian tribes to the west of the Mississippi. Cass later served for six years as American ambassador to France, and upon his return home he entered the Senate from Michigan, where he remained until the 1848 presidential campaign.

The man chosen to be the Democrats' vice presidential candidate was General William O. Butler of Kentucky. He was no stranger to Taylor, having commanded the Volunteer Division at Monterrey. By no means, however, was that assignment his only accomplishment. Born in 1781, Butler was also a veteran of the War of 1812 but as a junior officer. He had attained one great distinction: he had been aide-de-camp to Andrew Jackson at the Battle of New Orleans in January 1815. He had also served as a congressman from Kentucky from 1839 to 1843.

· · ·

The 1848 election also spawned a third party, the Free-Soil Party, whose motto was "Free Soil, Free Speech, Free Labor, and Free Men." Unlike the Liberty Party of the 1844 presidential election, it did not advocate the abolition of slavery where it already existed. In essence the Free-Soilers subscribed to the spirit of the Wilmot Proviso of 1846, a proposal put forth in Congress by David Wilmot of Pennsylvania. Its immediate objective was simply to ensure that any territory gained as a result of the Mexican War would be free, with no slavery permitted. Though the Wilmot Proviso had failed enactment into law, it had become a rallying cry for the Free-Soilers.

The new party's membership was polyglot. It began with antislavery elements in the Democratic Party, including the Barnburner faction from New York led by former president Martin Van Buren but also antislavery Whigs and former Liberty Party adherents. Meeting in Buffalo, the Free-Soilers nominated Van Buren for president and Charles Francis Adams for vice president. But unlike the Liberty Party, which in 1844 had cost the Whigs enough votes in New York to throw the state to Polk, the Free-Soil Party was not expected to exert a decisive influence because its members were drawn about equally from both the Whigs and the Democrats. The spectacle of a Democratic former president, Van Buren, opposing the Democratic Party, however, was dramatic, and the impact of that remained to be seen.

. . .

The Whig strategy for the 1848 election fit in exactly with Taylor's wishes: he planned to say as little as possible, leaving the bulk of the campaign to be conducted by surrogates, especially Thomas Ewing in Ohio and Thurlow Weed in New York. It was a sensible scheme because Taylor had not improved much in his propensity to commit political blunders. In one instance, it was as much a matter of the recipient of one of his letters, George Lippard, that caused pain among Whigs. Lippard had no credentials as a politician; he was, in fact, a sensational novelist, not of the best reputation. In July, Taylor told him, "I am not a party candidate, and if elected cannot be President of a party, but the President of the whole people."[12]

Because Taylor continued to insist on his independence from Whig straitjackets, the Whigs once more began to grow uneasy about his Whig convictions. The result, as in the period before his nomination, was that Taylor was induced to write another Allison letter. In this instance, unlike the first such missive, the original author is unknown. It was most likely Thomas Ewing. But never mind; it was the candidate who signed it. That was what counted.

With issues so mixed, and with neither major party committed to slavery or antislavery sentiments, the election became largely a local issues affair. In the South, for example, the Whig organization was strong in Georgia but weak in Alabama and Mississippi. Toward the end, Crittenden once more forsook his own gubernatorial campaign and took over Taylor's election effort. He played his role masterfully.

The key to the election was a trio of states—New York, Pennsylvania, and Ohio. Together they controlled 79 electoral votes out of a total of 146 needed to win. As it turned out, Taylor carried New York and Pennsylvania but lost Ohio.

In the final count, Taylor and Cass each carried fifteen states. Taylor, however, had carried more electoral votes: 163 to Cass's 127. Taylor also won the popular vote: 1,360,099 to 1,220,544.[13]

The news of his election reached Taylor by a circuitous route. It was sent by telegraph as far as Memphis, where the line ended, and from there was carried aboard a paddle-wheel steamer named, by coincidence, the *General Taylor*. When Taylor received the news, he showed no emotion at all. There were enough reasons to be less than exultant, but he resolved to do his duty.

Taylor had insisted that he would accept the presidency only if drafted by all the people. In the end it was not quite so. He had been drafted only by the Whigs, who were desperate for a winner. It was as a Whig that Old Rough and Ready was elected president of the United States.

9

Inauguration and Early Days
in the White House

Zachary Taylor had been elected president, but his inauguration was four months away.[1] In the meantime, he would still be a major general in the U.S. Army. Before assuming the presidency he would have to resign his commission, yet he was in no hurry. He wished to retain his pay and allowances as long as possible. In his letter to President Polk, he asked that his resignation be made effective as of January 31, 1849. That date, Polk wrote sniffily in his diary, was about the time that Taylor would leave his plantation at Baton Rouge and head for Washington.[2]

In the meantime, General Scott saw a potential awkwardness in Taylor's status as both president-elect of the United States and his own military subordinate. Scott therefore did a sensible thing. He himself took a sabbatical as general-in-chief and confined his command to that of the Eastern Department, leaving Taylor as commanding general of the Western. When Taylor's resignation should become effective, Scott would resume overall authority.

. . .

One day Taylor met his political rival Henry Clay for the first time. Clay happened to be a passenger on a Mississippi steamer heading from New Orleans for Washington, and it made a routine stop at Baton Rouge. Taylor had come aboard to see off two guests who had been staying at Cypress Grove. On the way into the main saloon, Taylor spied Clay sitting at a dinner table. Taylor faced Clay, bowed, and continued on his way. Clay ignored him until his dinner partner, sensing a gaffe, remarked, "Mr. Clay, that is General Taylor."

Clay's whole demeanor changed. He left the table and followed Taylor into the social hall, extending his hand, which Taylor warmly took. "General," Clay said, "you have grown out of my recollection." Taylor's answer was quick. "You can never grow out of mine."[3]

Today such an incident seems incredible. Taylor was the country's hero, the man who had just defeated Clay in his last political campaign and under whom Clay's son had died at Buena Vista. Yet Clay did not recognize Taylor when he saw him. The incident also casts light on the mercurial nature of Henry Clay, who could throw fits of rage when frustrated but, when calm, become the perfect gentleman. Nobody expected Clay, who was returning to the Senate, to be a staunch Taylor supporter. But their mutual aloofness was political, not personal.

• • •

In early December 1848, the Taylor family celebrated a joyous occasion in the marriage of the youngest daughter, Betty, to Colonel William W. S. Bliss, Taylor's very capable aide. It could not have been a more fortuitous connection. Taylor would need both Betty and Bliss in the White House, Bliss for writing orders, polishing letters, and providing advice, Betty to serve as the president's hostess. Margaret Taylor, who had made a bargain with God promising to eschew public appearances if her husband returned safely from Mexico, would reside with her husband in the White House but would live quietly upstairs. With the newly married couple on hand, Taylor would have the services of both daughter and son-in-law.

• • •

In spite of other activities to hold his attention, Taylor's most important chore during the interregnum was to select a cabinet. Six positions needed to be filled—secretary of state, secretary of the Treasury, secretary of war, attorney general, secretary of the navy, and post-master general. In addition to these six, Taylor and the Whigs decided to add another cabinet position, that of secretary of the interior.

The selection of a cabinet would have been difficult enough under any circumstances, but Taylor's problem, as a political outsider, was particularly so. And despite the general assumption that he would be a pawn in the hands of his advisers, Taylor was determined to be his own man, independent of extreme Whiggery. He would make his own, independent choices.

The result was a stream of messages to and from Washington, New York, and Baton Rouge. All this meant delay. Taylor was deliberate, and Ethan Allen Hitchcock, visiting Baton Rouge in late December, recorded in his diary that Taylor had not yet selected even one of his future cabinet members.

Hitchcock, always critical of Taylor, was at least partially misinformed. By that time Taylor had selected at least one cabinet member, Senator John M. Clayton of Delaware, to be secretary of state. He had not, it must be admitted, so informed Clayton before he left Baton Rouge.

Clayton had not been Taylor's first choice; his preference had been John Crittenden, whom Taylor wanted to have available in Washington in any capacity, as secretary of state, back in the Senate, or even as attorney general, a position he had once held.[4] Crittenden, however, believed that his election as governor of Kentucky obligated him to serve his state in that capacity. There was nothing Taylor could do to persuade him otherwise.

Clayton, however, was an excellent second choice. At age fifty-two, besides his natural gifts as a speaker and excellent record as a public servant, he was also the favorite of Thurlow Weed and William Seward. More important, perhaps, was his long, close association in the Senate with Crittenden himself. Clayton did have his drawbacks, though they were not apparent at first. Long a widower raising two sons alone, he could see the younger (and more promising) son, Charles, wasting away from consumption before his eyes. That tragedy may have been the cause of his reputed heavy drinking. At the time of his appointment, however, that tendency had not yet surfaced; in fact he seemed to be drowning his sorrows in his work. So if Crittenden was not available, Taylor was happy to settle on Clayton.

· · ·

In late January 1849 President-elect Taylor began his long and last road to the White House. His wife, Margaret, did not accompany him, probably to avoid the three-week succession of ceremonies and dinners. Still bitterly unhappy that her prayers for Zack's defeat at the polls had not been favorably answered, she traveled separately. But always the good army wife, she eventually made her way to Washington to dominate the domestic side of the White House, much as she had always dominated her home.

Taylor's trip from Baton Rouge to Washington was unusually arduous, and it was well that Margaret Taylor was not along. As was the custom, he traveled by water, using the magnificent river system that binds the middle of the country. After leaving Baton Rouge on the *Sea Gull* on February 16, he soon transferred to· the *Ben Franklin*, which was bound for Cincinnati. On a stop at Madison, Indiana, Taylor was struck by a falling trunk, giving him a painful bruise in the side. The weather was foul, windy, and cold. The conditions did not, however, deter great crowds from turning out to meet him. It was in Cincinnati—and only there—that Taylor sent a telegraph to John Clayton formally offering him the position of secretary of state.

Leaving Cincinnati aboard the *Telegraph No. 2*, bound for Pittsburgh, Taylor's party found its way blocked by the frozen Ohio River. The party therefore disembarked near Moundsville, Virginia, and after a long trek were able to procure sleighs to continue the trip to Wheeling, Virginia, which they reached on February 20.[5] They took sleighs and coaches for the rest of the tedious journey by way of Cumberland, Maryland. After ceremonies in Baltimore, they arrived in Washington on February 23.

By then Taylor had come down with a severe cold and rested in bed for the next two days before, according to protocol, he paid his formal call on President James Polk. By this time the sixty-four-year-old Taylor was tired and showing his age.[6]

• • •

Polk, not surprisingly, was exceedingly unhappy about the prospect of Zachary Taylor's forthcoming inauguration. It was not that Polk desired another term in office; he was happy to honor his long-standing pledge to serve only one term in the White House. Furthermore, he was tired and sickly. But he was suffering the disappointment that any president feels when, after the end of his term, his party is voted out of office. The outgoing president cannot avoid the feeling that the vote is a reflection on his own administration. Add to that Polk's personal dislike of Taylor, built up over two years of mutual antagonism. Nevertheless, the president was doubly determined to go through the change of administration on a cordial note.

On Saturday, February 23, about the time that Taylor arrived in Washington, Polk held a meeting of his cabinet to discuss the protocol of meeting with the president-elect. At first his cabinet members, perhaps hoping to attain posts in the new administration, favored paying their respects to the incoming president upon his arrival in the city. Polk, however, forbade them to do so until Taylor called on him first, and then the individual cabinet members could pay their own calls on Taylor. The members immediately acceded to Polk's wishes, overriding the objections of Secretary of State James Buchanan, who rarely saw eye to eye with his chief.

At 1:00 PM, on Monday, February 25, Zachary Taylor arrived at the White House, and a messenger informed President Polk, who was on the second floor, that his successor was waiting for him on the ground floor. Polk hurried down, and the two men met for the first time.

It was a brief and formal affair. Taylor was accompanied by a small entourage that included not only Clayton but also Jefferson Davis, now a U.S. senator from Mississippi. Polk was soon joined by his wife and two nieces. Apparently the atmosphere was friendly on the surface; Polk later recorded that he had received his guest with "courtesy and cordiality." In any event, Polk invited Taylor to dine at the White House on Thursday. Taylor said he would come if his health permitted.[7]

Three nights later, Taylor's health having cooperated, he and a small group joined Polk at the White House. Margaret had not yet arrived. The guests came from both parties—Millard Fillmore, Jefferson Davis, Senator John Bell, and the mayor of Washington. Taylor's dinner partner was Mrs. Sarah Polk; Polk himself "waited on" Mrs. George M. Dallas, wife of the outgoing vice president. With evident satisfaction, Polk recorded that "it passed off well. Not the slightest allusion was made to any political subject." The dinner broke up between nine and ten o'clock.[8]

. . .

Taylor had met his future secretary of state, John Clayton, for the first time immediately after arriving in Washington. It was well that Clayton had accepted the position and was on hand because Taylor benefited immeasurably from the assistance of the knowledgeable senator in making the remaining six appointments to his cabinet. All this had to be done in eleven days.

In most of the rest of his selections, as with Clayton, Taylor found himself forced to take his second choice. He was unable, for example, to persuade the distinguished Philadelphian Horace Binney to be secretary of the Treasury, and was forced to settle for another Philadelphia lawyer, William M. Meredith. Abbott Lawrence, a New England manufacturer, passed up the offer of secretary of the navy. The position was accepted by William Ballard Preston, a respectable man and one who was intensely loyal to Taylor but who had little knowledge of the navy and less desire to learn. Preston's interest and expertise was politics. Yet the navy would not present a problem to the Taylor administration. George W. Crawford immediately accepted his appointment as secretary of war and appeared to be a good choice.

The appointment of Reverdy Johnson of Maryland as attorney general received mixed reviews. On the favorable side, Johnson was the one appointee who really desired the position, and he has been described as the most diligent of any member of Taylor's cabinet. He was, however, criticized for immersing himself too much in detail. Regardless of that judgment, Johnson's influence on Taylor and his cabinet would be tremendous.

Of the remaining positions, the postmaster generalship, traditionally given to an influential politician who had helped the cause, went to Jacob Collamer after the post had been declined by Thomas Ewing of Ohio. Ewing was happy, however, to head the newly created Department of the Interior. The position resembled the postmaster generalship in one respect; both offices were rich with patronage, a field at which Ewing was a past master.

It was a respectable but lackluster cabinet. Not one position had been filled by a national figure. In the absence of Crittenden, Taylor might have asked Henry Clay to be secretary of state, thus lending some prestige to the cabinet. But despite their friendly meeting on the boat at Baton Rouge and a subsequent exchange of cordial letters, Taylor did not call on Clay's services, though in person he treated the Great Compromiser with respect and consideration.

Herein lay a weakness in Taylor's future conduct of the presidency. Perhaps because of his determination to be a president of all the people, Taylor did not make full use of the support of the prominent members of the Whig party, much as they could have helped him. He refused to confide in established figures such as Clay, Webster, or John Bell. Nor did he court Whig members of Congress.[9]

· · ·

On March 5, 1849, an unhappy but resigned former president James K. Polk wrote in his diary, "General Taylor is, I have no doubt, a well-meaning old man. He is, however, uneducated, exceedingly ignorant of public affairs, and I should judge of very ordinary capacity. He will be in the hands of others, and must rely wholly upon his cabinet to administer the government."[10] Polk had just completed his carriage ride with Taylor from the Irving Hotel, where the Polks had spent the previous night, to the Capitol. Taylor's inauguration had been deferred one day from the traditional March 4, which fell on a Sunday. By then the goodwill that had at least seemed to permeate the White House the previous Thursday evening had been forgotten.

Taylor's inaugural address was innocuous enough. Before a crowd of twenty thousand at the East Portico of the Capitol, he expressed humility at being chosen to be chief magistrate of the Republic. He paid compliments to his future associates in government, to the Congress, and to the judiciary. He rendered more than the usual obeisance to the memory of George Washington and emphasized once again Washington's admonition against entangling alliances. In only one paragraph of a short address did he express concepts differing from Polk's philosophy, that is, in his according precedence in domestic issues to the Congress.

It shall be my duty to recommend such constitutional measures to Congress as may be necessary and proper to secure encouragement and protection to the great interests of agriculture, commerce, and manufacture, to improve the rivers and harbors, to provide for the speedy extinguishment of the public debt, to enforce strict accountability on the part of all officers of the Government and the utmost economy in all public expenditures; but it is for the wisdom of Congress itself, in which all legislative powers are vested in the Constitution, to regulate these and other matters of domestic policy. I shall look with confidence to the enlightened patriotism of that body. . . . [11]

Such deference toward Congress was foreign to Polk's basic philosophy of government, but what really upset him was a casual remark that Taylor made regarding the newly conquered territory of California, the attainment of which had been a keystone of the Polk administration.

Something was said which drew from General Taylor the expression of views and opinions which greatly surprised me. They were to the effect that California and Oregon were too distant to become members of the Union, and that it would be better for them to be an independent government. He said that our people would inhabit them and repeated that it would be better for them to form an independent government for themselves. These are alarming opinions to be entertained by the President of the United States. . . . General Taylor's comments, I hope, have not been well considered.[12]

Polk's observations on Taylor, doubtless written with an eye to history, were remarkably bland compared to his personal feelings toward the man whose election had represented a complete failure of Polk's efforts to arrange a Democratic successor to himself. There was nothing, however, that the former president could do about it. When they reached the Irving Hotel, Polk left the carriage with a polite, pro forma wish for success.

Taylor continued on to the White House, which he expected to be his home for the next four years.

• • •

Zachary Taylor's first few weeks in office were crammed with official engagements. There were formal calls, for example, from the diplomatic corps. Since the informality of the times gave the president little or no protection from the intrusions of the public, he was plagued by office seekers, who felt free to walk in off the streets at will; the bolder ones even disturbed him at work. He gave them all at least a few minutes. Not that a person making a request necessarily got what he wanted. Those attempting to exert pressure or offer bribery, no matter how subtle, were readily ousted from Taylor's presence. Old Zack felt that he must at least receive any citizen who desired his ear, but he was not obliged to comply with what was asked of him.

There were also an unusual number of funerals to attend. One such event, totally unexpected, was the memorial service for Taylor's predecessor, James K. Polk, who died only four months after leaving the White House. More memorable, however, was the funeral of Dolley Madison, the eighty-one-year-old widow of the fourth American president, James Madison. Mrs. Madison has been remembered

in American lore principally for her courage in saving the portrait of
George Washington when the British descended on and burned the
White House in 1814. But her importance transcended that one
spectacular deed. She had played an active role in her husband's administration, and after his death she had settled in Washington,
where she had been the grande dame of society for many years. It
was at Mrs. Madison's funeral that Taylor coined a new term for the
American lexicon: "First Lady." That reference may not have sat well
with the other two prominent widows living in Washington. Mrs.
John Quincy Adams was one, and Mrs. Alexander Hamilton, who
considered herself on a par with widows of presidents, was the other.
Nonetheless, Taylor's phrase was universally approved and accepted,
though it came to apply solely to the wives of presidents.

In the meantime, the Taylors had settled down in the White
House and lived as much as they could as if they were back in Baton Rouge. With them lived William and Betty Bliss. Rebecca
(Becky) Taylor, Zack's niece, spent much time in the White House
while she attended school in the city. In the upstairs quarters of the
White House, Margaret Taylor ran a congenial and welcoming establishment, and since relatives abounded, guests were almost always present. Margaret, however, remained true to her resolve to
shun public life, a decision that caused the pampered members of
Washington society to begin circulating rumors about her. She was
said to be a recluse, a pipe-smoking bumpkin. Never mind the fact
that Margaret had come from a genteel Maryland family before
marrying Taylor, himself a wealthy man. The Taylors were aware of
these rumors, but that knowledge had no effect on the Taylor family life. Margaret's daughter Betty—vivacious, charming, and
capable—was queen on the ground floor of the Mansion but not in
the family apartments above.

In person, Taylor's personality sat well with the people of Washington. Since the president was not restricted in his movements by
security people, he was able to get away from the White House and
all its hubbub by taking long recreational walks around the city,
sometimes for remarkable distances. His attire became familiar to

the people on the street; his black silk hat habitually sat on the back of his head, and his clothes, by his own preference, were large and unfashionably comfortable. The habits Taylor had developed commanding armies in the field had not left him. One evening Taylor passed Henry Clay on the street and was offended when Clay, lost in thought, failed to greet him. Taylor, always touchy in such matters, later expressed his resentment, at which Clay apologized profusely.

Living conditions in the White House could have been better. The house needed paint and the roof leaked. The intense heat, for which Washington is famous, was exacerbated by the humidity. The filled-in soil that exists between the White House and the Potomac today did not exist in 1849, and the White House was close to the marshes at the edge of the river.

These conditions, annoying though they were, bore more significance than mere discomfort; they could spawn disease. During the summer of 1849, reports came in of a cholera epidemic creeping up from the south into the Midwest. By May, the scourge had reached as far north as Wisconsin, having taken the lives of 10 percent of the populations of both St. Louis and Cincinnati. If that epidemic should turn eastward, Washington would be a dangerous place indeed to live. That situation was not certain to come about, but so severe was the epidemic nationally that in July Taylor, not a particularly religious man himself, proclaimed a day of prayer.

During the summer Taylor, possibly because of this threat, decided to make a trip to Pennsylvania and New York, the official objective of which was to familiarize himself with conditions in the North, which were largely new to him. He was particularly interested, he said, in the needs of agriculture and industry. Despite the fact that gatherings of large numbers of people could be dangerous, he resolved to go ahead with his planned trip anyway.[13]

Taylor's small party included his son-in-law Dr. Robert Wood, but not Margaret. It left Washington by train on August 9. The itinerary was ambitious, with stops at Baltimore, York, Columbia, Lancaster, Mount Joy, Harrisburg, Pittsburgh, and Erie. From Erie the entourage planned to travel by steamer to Oswego, Albany, and down the Hudson to New York. From there the party would continue to Boston before returning to Washington by way of Philadelphia. All of this would take time, and Taylor did not plan to return to Washington until later in the fall. If his tour of the Northeast was intended to provide Taylor a rest from the strain of exposure to the public, it could not have failed worse. At every place the entourage stopped, great crowds gathered and gala events were lavishly planned. Taylor was an extrovert, and he enjoyed such gatherings, but they put a strain on his constitution, which was beginning to show signs of age. To add to the physical strain, the summer heat continued around the clock.

After a successful stop in Baltimore, which Taylor reportedly enjoyed, the train headed into Pennsylvania. At the state border the party was joined by Governor William F. Johnston, a sign that Taylor was learning the techniques of politics. The first significant stop in Pennsylvania was at Harrisburg, where Taylor conducted some important business. There he gave stern orders to Secretary of State John Clayton that the ports of New Orleans and New York were to be blockaded to prevent certain filibustering expeditions— small private invasions—from sailing to Cuba. But at Harrisburg the president's series of illnesses began to set in. He began to suffer from diarrhea and vomiting, which he attributed to a change of water. Dr. Wood administered medicines that seemed to ease Taylor's condition, and the party continued on.

Even in the worst stages of his illness, Taylor refused to allow his discomfort to curtail his activities. In Pittsburgh he gave a long speech significant for its support of protective tariffs—a Whig preoccupation. North of Pittsburgh, in Mercer County, the president met with a group of Free-Soilers from nearby Ohio and assured them that "the people of the North need have no apprehension of the further expansion of Slavery."[14] Here Taylor was setting forth a firm conviction. A slaveholder himself, who intended for his own economic reasons to keep his property, he was personally opposed to the institution in principle. He would not disrupt the Union by trying to abolish slavery in states where it already existed, but he would not allow its expansion into the new territories.

It was at Waterford, south of Erie, on August 24, that Taylor's illness hit him hard. The diarrhea and vomiting returned, this time with a fever and the "shakes." Dr. Wood removed the president to Erie, put him to bed, called in a consultant, and considered the condition serious enough to send word for Margaret to join him. She set out at once to be at his bedside. Five days later, however, Taylor had recovered sufficiently that Dr. Wood advised Margaret that the emergency had passed. When she received Wood's message in Baltimore, she returned to Washington. The presidential entourage was scheduled to continue its journey, although a little late, on September 1.[15]

At this point, the president's associates succeeded in convincing him that he should cut his schedule short. He could go as scheduled through New York but should cancel plans for Boston. Accordingly, the party left Niagara Falls on September 6 in a side-wheeler, leaving from Lewiston, just below the falls. Steaming across Lake Ontario, the party debarked at Oswego, where it was met by representatives of Thurlow Weed. From there it went by train to Albany, where Taylor was deemed strong enough to attend a state dinner. That activity, however, only confirmed the president's weakness. He was exhausted. He returned home by train.

Some men might be frightened by such an experience, but Taylor was made of stern stuff. He enjoyed a speedy recovery and was soon apparently fit. By the time that Congress returned to Washington in early December, he showed no signs of his recent indisposition.

Taylor's foray to the North admittedly fell short of maximum expectations. However, his activities along the way were significant because they showed a growing political sophistication. Ominous as the trip was regarding Taylor's health, it demonstrated that he was learning his job.

10

California and New Mexico

Zachary Taylor may have entered the White House untutored in the intricacies of politics, but he brought a set of convictions that he would doggedly pursue. One of these beliefs was opposition to the expansion of slavery into the territories recently acquired as the result of the Mexican War and the 1846 agreement with Britain over Oregon. The idea of moving slavery into these territories entailed needless controversy, he thought. He was convinced slavery would not be economically feasible in New Mexico and California and that the Wilmot Proviso was therefore moot. Other political leaders disagreed, sometimes violently. As a result the slavery issue would affect all issues addressed by Taylor's presidency.

Two problems raised by the acquisition of new territories would become matters of controversy. First was the status of the newly acquired lands. Would they become territories pending statehood, as was the usual case, or could some of these territories enter the Union as states immediately?

Second, would they be admitted, whether states or territories, as slave or free?

A third issue did not involve new territory: it had to do with the states where slavery already existed. It concerned the responsibility of the people of the North to return slaves that had escaped from their southern masters. A Fugitive Slave Act had been on the books since 1793, but the slaveholders of the South desired a new one with more teeth.[1] The new Fugitive Slave Act was immensely unpopular in the North and a cause for friction between Taylor and his Whig associate Henry Clay. Taylor disliked it, but Clay considered it part of a broader compromise package.

Even foreign affairs were affected by the slavery controversy. The normally peripheral matter of American filibustering expeditions—seizing control over local governments in the Caribbean and Central America—came into play. Some of these ventures, especially those directed toward Cuba, were supported by southerners hoping to bring new territories into the Union as slave states.

These issues did not arise one after another; they ran concurrently throughout Taylor's term in office. The only one that was immediate, however, was the status of California. The controversy was nearly two years old at the time of Taylor's inaugural.

The vast territory of California was sparsely populated. When it was first occupied by the United States in late 1846, it boasted only about ten thousand Caucasians and perhaps eight thousand Indians. General Stephen Kearny had reached San Diego in December 1846 and established formal military rule, under which the occupation of California was administered during the remainder of the Mexican War. Military rule was inevitable while the United States and Mexico were still officially at war, but when the Treaty of Guadalupe Hidalgo was ratified in the spring of 1848, military rule was no longer necessary. Nevertheless, no provision for civilian government had been made. So long as the region remained quiet, though, that situation created no immediate emergency.

The period of relative quiet was shattered, however, at about the time that Zachary Taylor, at Baton Rouge, was deciding to run for president. In January 1848, a man named James W. Marshall discovered flecks of gold in the American River, a spot not far from the major trading post named Sutter's Fort. The word came as a shock to Sutter, and the trader did everything in his power to keep the matter secret. Heretofore he had enjoyed a comfortable business providing supplies to overland travelers from the East, but now he sensed (correctly) that his lands would soon be inundated with gold seekers if the word got out.

Unfortunately for Sutter, the word did leak out. It went slowly at first. But once reported in the press, the discovery did not stay low-key for long. By April, even before the ratification of the Treaty of Guadalupe Hidalgo made California officially part of the United States, it was estimated that three-quarters of the population of San Francisco had emptied as men rushed for the mines. On July 14, the military governor, Colonel Richard B. Mason, inspected the area of the so-called Mormon diggings and reported some four thousand men of all descriptions, including foreigners and Indians, hard at work digging.

The lust for gold, Mason reported, had infected soldiers as well as civilians. Not only volunteers but regulars as well were deserting his small occupation force. Sailors from American warships and commercial vessels were jumping ship. The ports were becoming so crowded with ships bearing would-be prospectors that they were becoming unsafe, he advised. Yet they ignored the navigational dangers and continued to come in.[2] Under these conditions, it was obvious that military rule would have to come to an end much sooner than expected, and the question was becoming urgent as to what should be put in its place.

The people of California had long since reached the same conclusion. Military government, even as conducted by good men such as Generals Bennet Riley and Persifor Smith, was becoming onerous. Not only was it arbitrary; it also lacked enough administrators to perform the many functions that people expect of their government.[3] Accordingly, meetings began to spring up all over California, unconnected but pointed to one end: civilian rule.

Taylor, to the extent that he knew what was happening, was in full agreement with the citizens of California. Despite what James Polk had recorded in his diary on inauguration day, Taylor was anxious to install civilian government and to bring California into the Union. He also favored admitting it as a state rather than a territory. The swarming influx of immigrants had ensured that

California was more than qualified for statehood, at least in the matter of population.

As a general philosophy, however, Taylor conceded that the authority to grant admission of new states was a function of Congress, not the president. Nevertheless, he did not feel obligated to remain completely passive. Without waiting for Congress to act, he dispatched an agent to California only a month after being inaugurated. The instructions to the agent, Representative Thomas Butler King of Georgia, were vague. King was informed of Taylor's general desires but was given no specific marching orders.

King left Washington on April 3, 1849, and traveled to California by the usual route, by ship to Panama, thence across the isthmus, and again by ship, arriving at San Francisco on June 4. There he was surprised to learn that he was bringing the first news of Taylor's inauguration. More important, he found the people vastly disappointed to learn that Congress had done nothing to provide them a government. Absorbed with their own affairs, Californians had never imagined that their request for admission to the United States could be considered so important in the slavery issue.

Based on what they now knew, the people decided to act on their own. Though most of them were American citizens, American law had not yet been established, and they were still living under Mexican law. The rule of the alcaldes (mayors) was inconsistent and often oppressive. As an example of the confusion, King noted in his report that the customhouses of the ports had collected a million and a half dollars, but for lack of a functioning government the money had not been spent. The people were therefore setting up legislatures in San Francisco and elsewhere.

Action had actually already begun. A few days after King's arrival, General Riley came up from his headquarters and advised him that on June 3, the day before his arrival, Riley had called a convention to meet in San Francisco to form a state government. The people felt justified because California, unlike the other territories of the Union, possessed all the requirements for statehood. (It had even established the beginnings of trade with China.) The convention was scheduled to open on September 1, 1849.[4] This of course was what Zachary Taylor had in mind.

King did not play a role in the California Constitutional Convention. Shortly after his arrival, he set out on a reconnaissance of the state with Persifor Smith. At the end of the two-month tour, he came down with an unidentified fever that put him out of commission for two months. When the convention had finished its business in early October, King's main interest—and a source of pride to him—was the fact that the delegates, thirty-seven in number, included more members from slaveholding than nonslaveholding states,[5] and yet the convention had decided, by unanimous vote, that California should enter the Union as a free state.[6]

• • •

On December 4, 1849, Zachary Taylor issued his State of the Union message to Congress. It was a long, rambling affair, mixing the important with the trivial. In accordance with the formula accepted at the time, it began with a long discussion of the relationship of the United States to the outside world, especially Europe. With a straight face, he revealed an incredible blunder, his sending Andrew J. Donelson to Frankfurt am Main as the American minister to the German empire, only to discover, on Donelson's arrival, that the German empire did not exist. Donelson had therefore sent the papers of the legation to Berlin, where the United States had a minister to Prussia. Taylor rhapsodized over the United States' happy relationships with Britain and other countries. He included matters which were of no immediate concern to the United States but of interest because of its antiroyalist sentiments. One, for example, was an expression of support for the Magyars of Hungary in their futile efforts to break away from the Hapsburg empire.

In domestic affairs, Taylor's message mentioned the filibustering expeditions, the problems in drawing up the official boundary between the United States and Mexico (and the need for money to support same), the prospects for digging an Atlantic-Pacific canal across Nicaragua, the budget, the need for higher tariffs, the matter of brevet rank in the army, the opening of postal service in California, his philosophy regarding the relations between president and Congress, and finally—his southern foes should have taken notice—his determination to uphold the Union, come what may.

The president's treatment of statehood for California was brief.

No civil government has been provided by Congress for California, the people of that Territory, compelled by the necessities of their political condition, recently met for the purpose of forming a constitution and State government, which the latest advices give me reason to suppose has been accomplished; and it is believed they will shortly apply for the admission into the Union as a sovereign State. Should such be the case, and should their constitution be conformable to the requisites of the Constitution of the United States, I recommend their application to the favorable consideration of Congress.   •

In his conjecture that the people of California had drawn up their own constitution and were in the process of forwarding it to Congress, Taylor was correct. But the people of California, in their application for approval of their statehood, had made a serious error; they mentioned the prohibition of slavery in their draft constitution. By so doing, they made immediate approval by Congress an impossibility, given the determination of the southern senators to maintain a free state–slave state balance. Had the Californians omitted mention of that matter, they might have saved themselves a great deal of delay. They could then, as a state, have prohibited slavery.

Congress, therefore, included California in the slavery debate. Some southern senators, such as John C. Calhoun, pushed for its admission only as a slave state. More moderate senators, led by Henry S. Foote of Mississippi, preferred to hold the matter as a bargaining chip to secure future concessions in other matters. In the meantime the people of California gave up on the federal government and conducted their affairs under their new constitution just as if it had been approved.

Taylor's role in the California negotiations was finished. His main action had been the dispatch of King as his emissary early in his tenure. There was no doubt that California would eventually be admitted to the Union as a free state, but it would have to await the settlement of broader issues.

· · ·

Taylor had suffered little headache in the matter of statehood for California because the situation largely took care of itself. When it came to dealing with New Mexico, however, the president was not allowed the luxury of standing on the sidelines and watching things happen. He would soon be up to his ears in controversy, and it was here that he showed his greatest determination or, his critics contended, his petulance.

The reason for the difficulty in establishing New Mexico as a state lay to a large extent in the ongoing dispute between the inhabitants of that territory and the Texans, who claimed areas that nobody had ever conceded to them and over which they actually exercised no physical control. The disputed region consisted of a strip of land on both sides of the Rio Grande above El Paso and stretching northward to the river's headwaters near the town of Santa Fe. The more aggressive of the Texans also claimed ownership of Santa Fe itself. They were fighting a losing battle.

The Texans had tried to take Santa Fe before. Back in 1841, in fact, the independent Republic of Texas had sent an expedition to Santa Fe, then part of Mexico. The expedition had ended in disaster. All the members of the invading Texan force were killed or taken prisoner. Despite that fiasco, the Texans had never relinquished their claim. President Taylor considered the disposition of lands taken from Mexico to be a federal issue. The Texans, on the other hand, insisted that the dispute was between themselves and the sparse population of New Mexico. There the battle lines were drawn.

At the time of Taylor's inauguration, the lands formerly belonging to the Mexican state of New Mexico were solidly under United
States control. No change had occurred since General Kearny, in
the early fall of 1846, had proclaimed New Mexico as part of the
United States. Like California, New Mexico was still under military rule, despite the fact that President Polk, who had seemed
overly inclined to conciliate the Texans, had denied that the federal
government possessed any authority regarding the matter. Politically the issue was at an impasse.

The military commander in New Mexico in 1849 was Brevet
Lieutenant Colonel John M. Washington, the officer whose artillery
battery had so effectively stopped the attack of Santa Anna at the
Narrows at Buena Vista. Naturally Washington rejected the claims
of the Texas authorities and in so doing had distinct advantages. He
was on the spot with a force of United States troops, whereas the
Texas governor, George T. Wood, was eight hundred miles away in
Austin and possessed no physical presence in the area under dispute. Washington was a strong, determined man; he would not be
pushed around. Thus when Governor Wood sent Spruce M. Baird
as an agent to Santa Fe with documents saying that Texas must regard as void all judicial and civil proceedings "inconsistent with her
laws," Washington treated both Baird and the documents with an
attitude bordering on contempt. Military rule, he said, would continue until he was otherwise ordered by the United States government. The stalemate, with Washington holding all the cards,
continued into the summer of 1849, months after Taylor's inauguration. At that time Baird gave up and returned to Austin.[7]

The people of New Mexico, not surprisingly, were dead set
against conceding any territory to Texas. In October 1848—still
during Polk's term of office—they had met in Santa Fe and peti-
tioned Congress for admission to the United States as a territory,
free, not slave. Congress, however, was no more disposed to take action regarding New Mexico than it had been with California, and
the matter had essentially been dropped. Among other obstacles to
action, the disputed territory, as in California, was still operating

under Mexican law, which prohibited slavery. Under Texas law, it would become slave territory.

In September 1849, the people of New Mexico drew up another petition for admission to the Union as a territory. At about that time, however, President Taylor, for whatever reason, had concluded that New Mexico's entry as a state rather than a territory would be advantageous. When an officer was leaving Washington to join his regiment in Santa Fe, Secretary of War Crawford gave him a message advising that "if the people of New Mexico desired to take steps toward securing admission as a state, it would be his [Taylor's] duty not to thwart but to advance their wishes, since it was their right to ask for admission."[8] In so advising, Taylor had now taken the side of New Mexico in its dispute with Texas.[9]

Because of the distance between Washington and Santa Fe, matters moved slowly. Word could be sent with reasonable speed over water, but when it came to travel inland weeks would be needed for a message to go from one capital to another. Thus Taylor remained optimistic over the prospects of New Mexico's attaining statehood all the way up to his submission of the State of the Union address in December 1849; in the same paragraph as that in which he mentioned statehood for California, he advised that the people of New Mexico would soon "present themselves for admission into the Union." In the meantime they would "have instituted for themselves a republican form of government laying its foundation in such principles and organizing its powers in such form as to them will seem most likely to effect their safety and happiness." Congress, he urged, should await their action and "abstain from the introduction of those exciting topics of a sectional character which have hitherto produced painful apprehensions in the public mind." And, as he was wont to do, Taylor ended the subject by citing George Washington.

I repeat the solemn warning of the first and most illustrious of my predecessors against furnishing "any ground for characterizing parties by geographical discriminations."

Taylor was sincere but naive. Shortly after he sent his message to Congress, the new governor of Texas, the fire-eating P. Hansbrough Bell, secured permission from the Texas legislature to use force to establish Texan claims in Santa Fe. He also sent an emissary to Washington to raise money to pay Texas's debts by selling land north of latitude 36° 30' to the federal government. Unfortunately, he used intemperate language in referring to Taylor.

Neither of Bell's actions came to fruition. The use of force was a bluff at best. It was one thing for the Texas legislature to pass a resolution and something else to put an expedition in the field. Force had been tried before, as noted, and failed abysmally. And in this instance the foe would not be a tottering Mexican regime, but the United States Army.

The emissary to Washington fared no better. When a Texas delegation confronted Taylor with a threat of secession, they met a rebuff that must have jarred even that group of swashbucklers. Detailed accounts of the meeting vary, but a colorful one is often repeated, as in this commentary in a magazine published in 1970.

> [Taylor] displayed the same stubborn determination that had characterized him as a general. Thus, when a group of Southern congressmen came to the White House and threatened secession unless they got their way on New Mexico and the fugitive slave law, he replied angrily that "if it becomes necessary I'll take command of the army myself and if you are taken in rebellion against the Union I will hang you with less reluctance than I hanged deserters and spies in Mexico."[10]

Things continued to move slowly, but the New Mexicans, in keeping with the instructions sent them by Taylor, drew up a state constitution by May 24, 1850, calling for entry into the Union as a nonslave state. Given the temper of Congress, New Mexico's proposal then sat before that body, one of a list of issues to be worked on and, it was hoped, on which compromise could be reached.[11]

• • •

That left the question of Utah, or Deseret, as the Mormon community called itself. In a way, the application of Brigham Young's community was easier for Congress to reject because of the stigma, as the rest of the country viewed it, of legalized bigamy. Even without that, however, Deseret's territorial claims were excessive. The community asserted its right to all the territory between the Sierra Nevada and the Rocky Mountains north of Mexico and south of Oregon. To top it off, it maintained that Deseret was entitled to an outlet to the Pacific Ocean, a strip of land traversing southern California. Faced with that, Congress simply placed the Deseret application on the table and later admitted Deseret under territorial status.

Thus the organization of the territories seized or bought from Mexico or secured by negotiation from Britain dragged on. Neither issue would be solved during the time of the Taylor administration. The entire matter had seemed to be a simple question; instead it was engulfed in the overriding, burning question of the time: the future of slavery.

11

Foreign Affairs

President Taylor and Secretary of State Clayton made a good team when it came to maintaining the position of the United States in the family of nations. Before entering office, Taylor had had little experience and apparently less interest in diplomatic matters, though he did his best to emulate the advice of his hero, George Washington, to avoid entangling alliances and to maintain the honor of the country. Clayton, on the other hand, came from Delaware, a state that bordered on the Atlantic Ocean, and if his main concern was not in the art of diplomacy as such, he was intensely interested in international commerce.

In addition, the personalities of the two men fit well. Their political philosophies were similar, and Clayton, a strong defender of the status quo, was slow to anger. But when he needed the mailed fist to support his policies, Clayton could turn to Taylor, who was quick, perhaps too quick, to threaten the use of force if he deemed the honor of the United States to be impugned.

Taylor and Clayton, upon taking office in March 1849, inherited a set of ongoing problems, all of them minor and some of them stretching over years. In most cases, especially with some disagreements with France, the problems became vexatious more from matters of personality—of misunderstandings or superior European attitudes—than because of the issues themselves.

Troubles arose from time to time between the United States and France, Portugal, Spain, and Cuba. Those disputes, however, were usually dispelled and forgotten in a short time, with no lasting effect. The most potentially dangerous disagreement with France was brought about largely by the personality of the French minister in Washington, Guillaume Tell Poussin, a onetime American army officer. Poussin seemed to feel that he enjoyed special privileges with the Americans and was a constant thorn in Clayton's side when the secretary was trying to organize the department in early 1849. Taylor finally declared Poussin persona non grata, much to the irritation of the French foreign minister, Alexis de Tocqueville. Old Rough and Ready was willing to go to war over the matter, but Clayton managed to calm the troubled waters.

One diplomatic matter that plagued Taylor throughout his administration had to do with Cuba and came to be known as the López affair, the implications of which far transcended the mere size of the forces involved.

The cause of this headache was Narciso López, a Venezuelan by birth and a onetime officer in the Spanish army. When Spain was ousted from the mainland of Central America in the 1820s, López settled in Cuba, which Spain still held, and became a landowner. Deprived for some reason of his holdings, he fled to the United States, where he set about planning an invasion of Cuba to retake not only his old estate but also to wrest control of the entire island.

López was a dynamic, charismatic man, and he attracted a group of roughneck followers. His plan for colonizing Cuba received a friendly reception among many men in the South who, recognizing that the admission of California as a free state to the Union was inevitable, were looking for ways to add more slave states to the Union. (The institution of slavery had never been abolished in Cuba under Spanish rule.) Among López's supporters was John Quitman, governor of Mississippi and one of Zachary Taylor's brigade commanders at Monterrey.

By August 1849, when President Taylor was making his unfortunate trip to Pennsylvania, López had gathered an organization of some six hundred men. It was a small force with which to invade an island the size of Cuba, but López was counting heavily on an uprising of the people against the Spanish regime and their flocking to his banner. Clayton learned of these preparations, however, and being quite familiar with Taylor's determination to enforce the Neutrality Law of 1818, informed the president, who was at that moment resting in Lancaster. Taylor issued a proclamation denouncing such activities as "criminal" with the result that warships dispersed López's trainees, some of whom were at Round Island in the Mississippi River and others in a separate group in New York Harbor. That action put an effective end to López's first filibuster.

The problem, however, was far from solved, for López was a man not to be underestimated. Within a few months, in early 1850, he had organized another filibustering attempt, this time, he hoped, with the help of Mexican War heroes. He approached both Robert E. Lee and Jefferson Davis, but both men demurred. Not without anguish, however, because López was offering very generous remuneration.[1]

Again, however, word of López's plans leaked out, this time reaching the ears of the Spanish minister to Washington, Angel Calderón de la Barca, who notified Clayton. Now, however, López had developed a plausible cover plan: he claimed that his three ships (one steamer and two sailing ships) were headed for the Central American isthmus, where they would cross to the Pacific and continue on to California. The United States government could take no direct action against a legitimate voyage such as that, but the navy, suspicious of López's story, sent vessels to patrol the waters off Cuba. Their suspicions proved well founded, and the navy picked up the two sailing vessels. The steamer, carrying López himself, had gone to Contoy, off the Yucatán, where Spanish authorities attacked them and captured about fifty. López barely escaped with his life and made his way back to Key West, Florida. Taylor instructed Clayton to arrest López and whatever men had escaped with him. He had them all put on trial for violating the Neutrality Law. The culprits were, much to Taylor's displeasure, acquitted by friendly southern jurors.[2]

At the same time, though Taylor took action against López and his fellow renegades, he still stood up for the rights of American citizens, even wayward ones. The forty or fifty filibusters seized by the Spanish navy at Contoy were in danger of being executed as "pirates." Here Taylor, against the advice of his entire cabinet except Clayton, sent an ultimatum to the Spanish government defending the prisoners on the basis that they had, as of the time of their capture, taken no overt action against Spain; they had been guilty only of *intending* to commit the crime. A Spanish court eventually released all but three and later those three as well. Taylor did not live to see the final outcome, but he had upheld the honor of the nation while at the same time holding his own citizens to an observance of the law.

As a matter of interest, López later launched one expedition too many, in 1851. Again banking on the support of the Cuban people, he found to his dismay that they had no intention of rising up to overthrow the Spanish government. He was captured and executed by garroting in the plaza of Havana that year.

• • •

The greatest accomplishment of the Taylor administration in the foreign policy field was the treaty negotiated and signed between the United States and Britain called the Clayton-Bulwer Treaty.

By the middle of the nineteenth century, the interests of the United States and Britain, by and large, coincided. As the world's two leading nations in international commerce, they were both concerned with freedom of the seas and the promotion of trade. Their commonality of interests served as insurance against their ever going to war with each other. They might fuss and fume, as in the case of the Oregon border dispute of 1846, but somehow they would always find a peaceful way out of their disagreements. The need to maintain their basic friendship explains the very lavish paragraph extolling British-American friendship that Taylor included in the State of the Union address of December 1849.

All this did not, however, prevent the two countries from competing in certain areas of the world, especially in the Caribbean. The threat of British expansion in the Western Hemisphere was always bandied about the United States in instances such as the annexation of Texas in 1845, California in 1846, and possibly Cuba in 1849. The Monroe Doctrine, so emphasized in our children's textbooks, was far from an ironclad policy. The oceans are wide, and not even the energetic and growing United States could police the entire Western Hemisphere. Everybody knew that, particularly the United States and Britain.

When Clayton assumed office as secretary of state, he harbored a vision of a new era, one in which Britain's temporary dominion over the Caribbean area, maintained by commercial rather than military means, would be replaced or at least shared equally by the United States. President Polk and his secretary of state, James Buchanan, their eyes focused on the war with Mexico and westward expansion, had neglected, in Clayton's view, the threat to United States interests in the Caribbean, giving Britain almost a free hand in that region.

In 1849, spurred on by the flood of prospectors who were trying to make their way to the gold of California, the attention of both countries was directed to the possibility of building a canal across Central America. Such a canal would produce immeasurable benefits to whatever nation built it and, if internationalized, for all nations. The canal would cut off thousands of miles from a long and dangerous trip from the Atlantic coast of South America through the Strait of Magellan to the Pacific. It would bring in untold revenue. Its construction should be a boon to all trading nations. To that end, American companies, especially the Atlantic and Pacific Ship Canal Company,[3] had begun negotiations with the Nicaraguan government for the building of the canal.

The Americans were not alone. The British were also interested in the prospect of a canal across Nicaragua, or at least in ensuring that such a canal could not be built without their participation. This they had done by establishing a protectorate over a small area called the Mosquito Coast, named after a small tribe of Indians of that name. In early January 1848, they had also seized the Nicaraguan town of San Juan del Norte, claiming that it was part of the Mosquito territory. They had also installed a puppet, an Indian boy on whom they had conferred the impressive title of King George Augustus Frederick. The relationship of the British to the Mosquito Coast remained vague, but they always insisted that the Mosquito Coast was independent of Nicaragua, since the Miskitos had never succumbed to Spanish rule.

The British claim was weakened, however, because San Juan had not joined them voluntarily and had succumbed only after being put down in a seesaw fight. Not by coincidence would San Juan be the Atlantic terminus of any canal to be built along the most logical route across the isthmus. There the situation stood when the Taylor administration took office.

Negotiations to settle the issue were conducted in three localities: London, Washington, and Nicaragua itself. Despite Clayton's accusations, they had begun well before the 1848 election. The place where representatives of the two governments might reach a mutually acceptable agreement made no particular difference because any treaty would have to be ratified by the American Congress and the British Parliament.

The result turned out to be a three-ring circus. The negotiations in London proved to be meaningless and those in Nicaragua (if they could be called negotiations) were downright harmful to the cause. One reason for the confusion, beyond anyone's control, was the time it took for messages to travel between the three points of action. Thus each negotiator was left largely on his own, and the results were often contradictory.

With the change in the American administration, President Taylor appointed a new minister to London, Abbott Lawrence, to replace Polk's minister, the historian and previous secretary of the navy, George Bancroft. Lawrence, however, became seriously ill before leaving Washington, and in his absence Taylor was content for Bancroft to continue in the post. It is possible that Bancroft had somehow offended the British foreign secretary, Lord Palmerston, for that official claimed time after time that he was too busy to hold talks with Bancroft on the subject. Whatever the reason, Palmerston's attitude might be understandable; after all, the subject to be discussed was the proposal to reduce the British influence in Nicaragua. When Palmerston finally met with Bancroft, the foreign minister was the soul of cordiality, but very soon after the conversation began he was called away on another matter. The talks were never resumed.

In Nicaragua the situation was even worse, and the representatives of Britain and the United States played games of deception. The British representative, Frederick Chatfield, beat the Americans to the draw by securing a British warship to seize Tigre Island, a small piece of land on the Pacific coast that belonged to Honduras. Like the Mosquito Coast, Tigre Island was worthless except for the fact that it controlled the approach to the Pacific side of the prospective canal. Thus the British controlled both exits of the best canal route, even though the Americans had the inside track diplomatically with the Nicaraguans themselves. The shenanigans were not all one-sided. The Americans also contributed to the confusion. President Polk's representative to Nicaragua had been Elijah Hise, whom Taylor and Clayton had replaced with E. George Squire, a twenty-seven-year-old civil engineer. For some reason, however, Hise received no word (or so he claimed) that he had been replaced; he continued to function. Oddly, the government of Nicaragua did not inform him of his removal either, so both Americans, Hise and Squire, each believed himself to be representing the United States. Both men negotiated separate treaties with Nicaragua, each pledging that the United States would support, presumably by force, Nicaragua's claim to ownership of San Juan and the Mosquito Coast. It seems possible that, since the two agents were on hand informally, without formal portfolios, the Nicaraguans saw no objection to dealing with two of them. In any case, both treaties gave the Nicaraguans what they wanted.

This situation presented both advantages and disadvantages to Taylor and Clayton. The agreements negotiated in Nicaragua did, of course, do damage to American efforts to conduct talks with the British in a spirit of amity and cooperation. On the other hand, the existence of the treaties gave Taylor a justification to honor whichever one of them he chose. The Squire treaty was the one most likely to be used.

Washington, it turned out, became the only place where serious business could be conducted between Britain and the United States. The solution came in the person of a new British envoy, Henry L. Bulwer, who arrived in Washington in January 1850. Bulwer was ideal for the task. A graduate of Cambridge University, a onetime member of Parliament, and an experienced diplomat, he was friendly and outgoing, immediately popular in Washington. In addition, he genuinely wanted an agreement, even though he would interpret any agreement as he saw fit to protect the British hegemony over the Mosquito Coast.

It did not take long for Clayton and Bulwer, working together, to come up with a draft treaty. Clayton submitted it for Taylor's approval in early February 1850. Taylor looked it over and found the wording too vague for his taste, especially as it applied to the British protectorate over the Mosquito Coast. He returned it for reworking, and it was April before the two diplomats could make revisions and secure the approval of Palmerston's government. Taylor submitted this draft to the Senate and received its ratification on July 5, 1850. Taylor signed it and proclaimed its approval in what turned out to be his last official act.

The critical wording was as follows:

> Neither [Britain nor the United States] will ever obtain or maintain for itself any exclusive control over the said ship canal . . . that neither will ever erect or maintain any fortifications commanding the same . . . or occupy, or fortify,

or colonize, or assume, or exercise any dominion over
Nicaragua, Costa Rica, the Mosquito Coast, or any part of
Central America.[4]

The wording was negative, declaring only what the parties
would not do. On the other hand, it prevented a war between the
two countries and furthered the growing atmosphere of mutual
understanding. It also, regrettably, ensured that no canal would be
built across Nicaragua for the foreseeable future. Fifty years later,
the treaty would constitute a thorn in the side of President
Theodore Roosevelt in his efforts to build an American Panama
Canal.

12

The Great Debate

During the spring and early summer of 1850, three related proposals were being debated in Congress, particularly the Senate. One of these was the proposed admission of California to the Union as a territory or a state; a second was the future status of New Mexico, a more complicated matter; the third was the controversial proposal to strengthen the Fugitive Slave Law. Taylor, having made his requests for California and New Mexico statehood in his December message, conceded that these were matters for Congress to decide. He would have no direct role in any of these congressional debates, though his presidential veto power always made his attitude a matter of much concern to all in Congress.

The slavery issue dominated all the debates, but partisan politics also played a role. The American habit of viewing nearly all matters, particularly domestic, in the light of their impact on the next presidential election is nothing new. The posturings of the senators, especially among those with an eye on the White House, were varied because political parties had not yet taken on the almost totally sectional nature that would mark the scene a decade later. Thus there were southern Whigs such as Taylor; northern Whigs such as Daniel Webster and William Seward; southern Democrats such as Jefferson Davis or John C. Calhoun; and northern Democrats such as Lewis Cass.

These confused loyalties made for strange situations. For example, Taylor's staunchest ally in his argument favoring the immediate admission of California as a free state was not a Whig but a Democrat from a slave state, Senator Thomas Hart Benton of Missouri. Benton was already among those who opposed the expansion of slavery, and when it came to California he was doubtless influenced in supporting statehood ambitions by the fact that his son-in-law, John C. Frémont, had been nominated by the people of California to be one of its first two senators. Even without that incentive, however, Benton's philosophy of popular sovereignty ran close to Taylor's. On the other hand, Daniel Webster, a northern Whig, felt some affinity for the southern slaveholders. A friend of big business, Webster tended to view large plantations as much akin to businesses of the North, including the cotton mills of New England. His official position was aligned against the expansion of slavery, but he was far from rabid on the subject.

As of the middle of the nineteenth century, the trio of statesmen commonly thought of as political giants were nearing the end of their careers. John C. Calhoun of South Carolina was dying of consumption but determined to fight for southern rights to the last. Henry Clay, despite his seventy-one years and poor health, had still thought himself fit to run for president in 1848. Daniel Webster was sixty-eight years of age, and his hard drinking did nothing to improve his condition.

There were other participants, though they have not been remembered with the same respect as the "big three." One of these was William H. Seward of New York; another was Henry S. Foote of Mississippi, a one-term senator who led the southern charge against accepting the admission of California as a free state without exacting a price. Small in stature but strong in conviction, Foote would constitute a formidable obstacle to any one-sided concessions on the part of the South.

. . .

Of all the senators debating the future of the Union in 1850, Henry Clay, the Whig majority leader in the Senate, stood preeminent. Clay had founded the Whig party in 1834, soon after his trouncing by Andrew Jackson in the presidential election of 1832. In the 1836 election the Whigs had considered Clay, among others, but had finally settled on running several candidates, including the military hero William Henry Harrison, this time against Jackson's vice president and protégé, Martin Van Buren. The aura of Jackson had been too strong, however, and Van Buren had won. By 1840, with the country reeling from an economic depression, Harrison defeated Van Buren, only to die in office a month after his inauguration. But in two successive presidential elections in 1836 and 1840, the greatest Whig leader, Clay, had not been the party's nominee.

Clay's best shot for the White House had come when he was nominated by the Whigs in 1844. The election was a heartbreaker for Clay, as he lost to James K. Polk by a whisker. That election was the last time that a Clay candidacy had been taken seriously by anyone but himself, though he did not face that fact squarely. His effort to attain the Whig nomination in 1848 had been almost embarrassing. Still Clay was Mr. Whig, with stature unmatched in his role as the majority leader in the Senate.

Taylor and Clay should have been allies. Clay, like Taylor, was a slaveholder who nonetheless disapproved of the institution and opposed its expansion into the newly acquired territories. Clay could have been a bigger help to Taylor, for he had a genius for compromise, so necessary to promoting Taylor's programs. He was known admiringly as the Great Compromiser. But neither man seemed to be interested in such teamwork, so Clay operated independently in the domestic confrontations that raged during the spring and early summer of 1850. So visible was Clay on the national scene that conjecture arose in some quarters that Taylor was jealous of being upstaged by the old Whig warhorse.

In late January 1850, Clay proposed a set of measures that he hoped would win the grudging approval, if not enthusiasm, of both sides of the slavery question. California should be admitted immediately to the Union as a free state, but the rest of the recently acquired territories should remain as territories on a popular sovereignty basis.

In other words, whenever New Mexico and Deseret (Utah) should enter the Union, they should be allowed to come in as free or slave, depending on the choice of the people. The United States should purchase those parts of New Mexico claimed by Texas, no matter how shaky the Texan claim might be, in order to round out the future state of New Mexico to a viable entity. The slave trade, but not slavery itself, should be abolished in the District of Columbia—a sop to the Free-Soilers—but a much stronger fugitive slave law should be enacted as a sop to the South.

Taken together, this omnibus bill had no chance of passage; every faction could find some aspect to vote against. So the debate went on. To the North, the Fugitive Slave Bill was a particular anathema, because it required private citizens to participate and assist in the federal apprehension of runaway slaves. It effectively turned the entire northern population, of all colors, into one vast slave patrol. It gave federal recognition to what had heretofore been considered a matter for the individual states of the South.

On March 4, John C. Calhoun's last and one of his greatest speeches was presented before the Senate. It was distinguished not so much for its contents but for the clarity with which it summarized the southern point of view. Slavery, Calhoun warned, was the issue that might destroy the Union. "I have believed from the first that the agitation of the subject of slavery would, if not prevented by some timely and effective measure, end in disunion," he proclaimed. California, Calhoun went on, "will become the test question. If you admit her, under all the difficulties that oppose her admission, you compel us to infer that you intend to exclude us from the whole of the acquired territories, with the intention of destroying, irretrievably, the equilibrium between the two sections."[1] The only way to guarantee southern rights, Calhoun concluded, was an amendment to the Constitution of the United States restoring to the South "the power she possessed of protecting herself before the equilibrium was destroyed."[2]

It was Calhoun's last great effort, but he was unable to present it personally. Though he was present, he was so weak that he had to ask James Mason of Virginia to read it for him. Less than four weeks later, on March 31, 1850, Calhoun died.

The hope for compromise was still strong, however. On March 7, three days after Calhoun's speech, Daniel Webster made what was probably his most memorable speech, at least of his later years, the so-called Seventh of March Speech. Despite his age and poor health, Webster's presence that day has been described by some as "majestic" and by others as "bordering on arrogance for its self-confidence."[3] The most remembered of his words were the first: "I speak not as a Massachusetts man, nor as a Northern man, but as an American." He went on to speak with reason, with his main thesis the disaster that would befall the entire country if the Union were to break up. He decried the positions of the extremists, insisting that the nation's course must be characterized by "mutual charity and concessions." He warned his fellow northerners against unnecessary insults to the South and contended that slavery was not feasible in states such as California, thus making the Wilmot Proviso, such a banner to many northerners, unnecessary. The crucial point of Webster's oration, however, was in declaring his willingness to support the Fugitive Slave Law. This was a giant swing from the Webster who spoke so strongly against Calhoun and the nullifiers back in the Nullification Crisis of 1832–33.

Reaction to Webster's Seventh of March Speech was predictably varied. Calhoun, whom Webster assumed to be absent, was in the audience and rose to his feet to insist that, if the South were pushed into a corner, the Union could be broken. Webster answered that indeed it could, but "such a calamity would be a revolution."[4]

Others joined in. The poet John Greenleaf Whittier, as rabid an abolitionist as Calhoun was a southerner, wrote, more in sorrow than in anger, a poem, "Ichabod," depicting Webster as a traitor to the cause.[5] Others joined him. Nevertheless, the bulk of the reception to the Seventh of March Speech was favorable, particularly in the North. However, even Calhoun found much to praise in it. It played its part in the compromise that was to follow.

Not all the speeches in Congress were conducted with the same dignity as were those of Clay, Calhoun, and Webster. One episode, since it was solved without bloodshed, has its humorous aspects. It transpired between two hotheaded southerners, though men of different persuasion.

In mid-January, at about the time that Clay was putting together his omnibus bill, Mississippi senator Foote and Missouri senator Benton introduced bills whose provisions were diametrically opposite. Benton, probably the strongest Union man in the Senate, introduced a bill that would accept California as a free state but would also split Texas in two, thus maintaining the voting balance in the Senate. It would also give Texas adequate compensation for the New Mexico territory that Texas was claiming. Foote's bill would honor all of the Texan claims and even go so far as to reject California's statehood application and accept her only as a territory.

The confrontation seems to have been prompted as much by personal animosity as any contradictory pieces of legislation, and the conjecture was that Foote's cronies had designated him to cut Benton down to size. He was a good selection. Small, bald, and scrawny at age forty-six, he has been described as "afflicted with a patriotic form of the dance of St. Vidas."[6] Though a poor pistol shot, he had fought four duels, having been wounded in three. He was twenty-two years younger than Benton who, like Webster and Calhoun, was sixty-eight.

But Foote was assailing a tough man. Benton, a person of large stature, carried the distinction of having shot and wounded the formidable Andrew Jackson back in 1815 and somehow lived to tell the tale. Following that incident, though the wound caused Jackson pain for years, Benton and Jackson became close allies; it would be difficult to choose between them as to which was the more fearless. Benton's ego had been demonstrated when he had plotted with James Polk to get him appointed a lieutenant general.

Foote's attacks on Benton were only verbal but they occurred daily and were couched in strong language. Vice President Millard

Fillmore, presiding over the Senate, was distraught but unable to put an end to Foote's tirades. On April 17 Benton finally lost patience with Foote's attacks and, when the latter began his usual vituperation, rose and began approaching the Mississippian, who pulled a pistol and retreated down the aisle toward the front of the Senate chamber. Stopped once, Benton then saw the pistol. Rather than retreat, he thrust open his coat and continued in Foote's direction. "I have no pistols," he shouted. "Let him fire. Stand out of the way! Let the assassin fire!" Confusion broke loose, but enough levelheaded solons grasped both men and led them back to their seats.[7]

Foote, however, was no secessionist, despite his intransigent proslavery positions. On March 13 he submitted a set of compromise resolutions on the Senate floor, the most important of which would be the establishment of a committee of thirteen senators, chaired by Clay, to combine all the contrasting proposals, especially the statehood and fugitive slave proposals, into a single bill. The committee met and predictably came up with a program that looked very much like the original set of proposals that Clay had submitted a month before.

That attempt at compromise had an odd effect: it caused a rift between President Taylor and Senator Clay—or perhaps it would be better to say exacerbated the rift between them.

The dichotomy of views centered principally around two issues. One was that of the admission of California as a free state. In Taylor's mind, there was no reason in the world why California should not be admitted as a state without delay. To the practical politician Clay, who had to undergo the attacks by Henry Foote and others on a daily basis, the California issue had to be viewed as a bargaining chip to make a balanced compromise that the South could live with.

The other issue was the fugitive slave proviso, the real key to Clay's compromise. Heretofore slavery had been a state-by-state matter. According to this proviso it would be afforded federal recognition—and, if enforced, a strong recognition at that.

As the spring of 1850 turned into early summer, the lineup of political positions was strange, without a definite pattern. By normal procedures, though Taylor's closest ally should have been Clay, the Whig majority leader in the Senate, they were almost rivals. The chemistry between the two, however, was not right. The fault, in all likelihood, lay principally with Clay, who doubtless regarded Taylor as a political tyro. As the man who, in his own mind, should have been president himself, Clay could never subordinate his own views and position to that of a president-by-chance. Clay became, in fact, one of Taylor's problems.

Another man who should have been close to Taylor was Vice President Millard Fillmore, an experienced and respected politician, one who could balance Taylor's southern Whiggery with that of New York. But for some reason, Taylor did not care for Fillmore and, much to Fillmore's anguish, refused to bring him along as a partner.

The man who stepped into the breach left by Clay and Fillmore was Senator William H. Seward of New York, protégé of Thurlow Weed but a figure who had by now eclipsed the influence of his mentor. Seward, who sixteen years later would be remembered for his purchase of Alaska from Russia, was a calculating, devious sort of politician, but he was sincerely antislavery in his convictions. He made no effort to conceal his influence at the White House; in fact he exaggerated it. He took full credit for influencing Taylor, a slaveholder, to oppose the expansion of that institution into the newly acquired territories. Never mind that Taylor had come to the same conclusion on his own.

At one point, Seward's enemies took heart in the hope that his influence with Taylor was at an end. On March 13, Seward, who was adamantly against the efforts at compromise, made a speech in which he declared that the Constitution did not recognize slavery and that the issue should not dominate even the slave states because such a small percentage of their populations were slaveholders. Most memorable were the words that slavery was "only a temporary, accidental, partial, and incongruous" institution while freedom was "a perpetual, organic, universal in harmony with the Constitution." He pointed out that other nations such as Britain, France, and even Mexico had abolished slavery.[8]

Taylor was livid, perhaps less because of Seward's exact points than in his superior attitude in enunciating them. A senator visiting the White House reported that Taylor was "so excited that he stuttered." But Taylor soon cooled down, and a week later he and Seward were once more on cordial terms. The wily Seward knew how to warm the heart of the man in the White House: he presented Taylor with a silver currycomb for Old Whitey.[9]

While the great debate raged in the Congress, Zachary Taylor took an action that illustrates his faith that slavery was in no danger in the states where it already existed. In early June he instructed his son Richard to purchase a new plantation in an area less vulnerable to the flooding of the Mississippi. With it came eighty-five to ninety "good hands." Taylor estimated that the plantation, costing $115,000, would produce an income of $20,000 a year.[10]

13

The Death
of the President

There may have been no connection at all. The stress that the so-called Galphin scandal inflicted on President Taylor may have had nothing to do with his untimely death. The coincidence, however, is too close to ignore. Taylor's health had held up well for thirteen months in office despite many severe attacks on his administration's policies and even on him personally. When the integrity of his administration was impugned, however, observers began to notice that he was aging and looking tired. At the very least the Galphin affair provided a tragic atmosphere in the shadow of which the president attempted to deal with larger issues in his last days.

Taylor himself was guilty of no wrongdoing, unless his lifelong habit of placing excessive and sometimes unwarranted trust in his subordinates can be considered a cause for censure. But the actions of three members of his cabinet—Secretary of War George W. Crawford, Secretary of the Treasury William M. Meredith, and Attorney General Reverdy Johnson—are very much open to censure.

The incident that evolved into the Galphin scandal had its origins three-quarters of a century earlier, before the American Revolution. It began as a fairly routine claim submitted by a private citizen, George Galphin, against the British Crown, for his services in the course of certain land dealings with the local Indian tribes in Georgia. Any dealings of the white men with the Indians must be suspect, of course, but the British authorities honored the claim and promised to reimburse the plaintiff for his losses. The ink was hardly dry on the promise, however, before unrest against British rule began to break out in the Colonies. The British government, therefore, paid only the claims of those men who had remained loyal to the mother country. Galphin was not one of them. He had joined with the rebellious colonists, and he was among those not paid. At the end of the Revolutionary War, his claim was assumed by the state of Georgia.[1]

Georgia, however, was in no rush to cover the debts of the British government, and the claim sat on the shelf unpaid for years. It came up from time to time in the state Senate, and it was always approved in principle, but payment was always deferred because the state lacked the funds. In 1835 the United States government assumed the claim from Georgia but likewise held off immediate payment.

By this time George Galphin was long gone, but his heirs continued to press the suit. George Crawford, then a Georgia lawyer, had been representing the plaintiffs for about fifteen years when Zachary Taylor took him under consideration for a cabinet post. By that time President James K. Polk's secretary of the Treasury, Robert J. Walker, had declared the claim valid and paid the principal—$43,518.97—but not the more ambitious claim for the interest, which had grown to four times the size of the original principal. The heirs continued to press their claim for that as well.

How much Taylor actually knew and understood about the intricacies of Crawford's role in this matter is not clear. In later testimony, Crawford asserted that he had attempted to explain the possible embarrassment when Taylor (or his representative) was interviewing him for the cabinet. Taylor, Crawford later insisted, had waved the matter off, reasoning that the past was of little or no consequence.

In April 1850 the matter came to a head. The Galphin claim for the interest reached the desk of Secretary of the Treasury Meredith, who consulted with Attorney General Johnson. Johnson had the ultimate authority, and he approved the payment of interest, which had now swelled to the spectacular amount of $191,352.89. Crawford, as agent for the claimants, was legally due half of those proceeds.[2] Taylor, therefore, was placed in a position where his secretary of war had been awarded what was considered an unthinkable amount of money by the decision of two other members of his own cabinet.

Crawford, it has been pointed out, might have deflected the public criticism by waiving the payment. That, however, he refused to do. He was a practical man, and he realized that his position in the cabinet, no matter how prestigious, was only temporary. On the other hand, his award was technically legal, and it would make him a rich man. It is difficult to condemn Crawford for refusing to waive his fee, but the episode resulted in anguish for President Taylor.

Perhaps coincidentally and perhaps not, Taylor, at the urging of Senator William Seward, was already entertaining thoughts of replacing some if not all the members of his cabinet. Such a sweeping action was contrary to Taylor's habits, and his stewing over the prospect must have caused him great stress. The matter was active when July rolled around.

• • •

During the night of July 3, 1850, Taylor reportedly slept little, quite possibly wrestling in his mind with the Crawford dilemma facing him. Nevertheless, he was not inclined to allow a bad night to keep him from his duties and enjoyment. On the morning of the Fourth of July, he started his day by attending a school recital. He then went on to other things.

The big event of the day was a ceremony in the early afternoon at the site of the future Washington Monument, the laying of its cornerstone. The main speaker at the event was Senator Henry S. Foote, who delivered a long, pious diatribe about sectional understanding. Taylor sat through the two hours of rhetoric but afterward admonished the champion of southern rights that his conduct should live up to his words. The Washington heat was at its worst, but when the monument ceremony was finished, Taylor went off for a walk. He toured the city in the broiling sun before heading back to the White House. In the course of the day he ate large quantities of green apples and cherries, washed down with ice-cold milk. As a result, he finished the day with symptoms of severe gastroenteritis, which did not at first seem serious. Taylor's symptoms, the doctors noted, were very much like those he had suffered the previous September on his trip to Pennsylvania.

What the doctors did not know—and could not know—was that Taylor's malady would soon lead to something worse, infection. Nobody knew the exact nature of the bug (or bugs), and they lumped all such maladies under the name of "cholera morbus." The fact is that Washington's water and sewage systems were still primitive and unsanitary; other prominent people—Clayton, Seward, Crawford, and Bliss—were all sick with something like Taylor's condition at that very moment.[3] In no case was anyone sure of the nature of the disease.

By Saturday, July 6, Taylor was thought to be getting better. He went to his desk and signed the Clayton-Bulwer Treaty as well as sending a letter thanking some friend for the gift of a couple of fine salmon. But while the president seemed to be getting better, the infection was spreading. The doctors, who now included four prominent physicians,[4] treated the patient as best they could, with calomel and quinine, but nothing could be called effective.

Still there was no public alarm at the president's condition. That Saturday, while Taylor was enjoying his brief respite, Congress was meeting to debate the Galphin claim and even voted by a close margin to censure Taylor for his role in the scandal. Soon, however, Taylor's condition sank, and by Sunday he dropped a remark predicting his own death. At one hour he would be reported as improving, a cause of celebration, and then bad news would follow.

By 2:00 PM on Tuesday, July 9, it was obvious that Taylor was sinking and would not recover. The family had been gathered for the last moments. At 10:35 PM he died. His last reported words were,

> I am about to die—I expect the summons soon—I have endeavored to discharge all my official duties faithfully. I regret nothing, but am sorry that I am about to leave my friends.[5]

The scene was unusually pathetic because of Margaret Taylor's pitiful grief. At her side was the Taylors' daughter Betty Bliss, who was no help because she was nearly prostrate. Margaret Taylor had her own ideas about the disposition of her husband's body. She refused to permit embalming, and after the casket was closed, she demanded three times that it be reopened to permit her a final look. But the life was over.

• • •

Meanwhile, the word was slow in reaching Congress. The Senate was in the midst of a debate over states' rights—what else?—shortly after Tuesday noon when the word came of Taylor's impending death. Vice President Millard Fillmore, presiding, received a message but did not immediately reveal its contents. Instead he descended from his seat to the Senate floor and spoke quietly to Webster, Clay, and Cass. Webster took it upon himself to make the announcement, but according to Senate rules he could not get the floor right away. When he did, he rose to his feet and announced the "appalling news . . . that in a few hours the President would be no more." Webster was choked with emotion, and he was joined by many others.

It was Fillmore's turn. Expressing himself as "overwhelmed with grief," he set the next day at noon for his own swearing in. It was a sign of quieter times that the United States could be allowed to go without a president for a half day or more before a new one was inaugurated.[6]

From that time on, at least for a while, party rivalry was set aside. Members of Congress from both houses and from all sections of the country vied with one another in singing the praises of the departed president. The speeches were not hypocritical. Many people disapproved of Taylor's policies; some were puzzled by them; and others, especially in the South, felt threatened by them. But in death all recognized the value of Taylor as a man, and he was once more the national hero.

• • •

The funeral arrangements were elaborate. Taylor was only the second president to die in office. And Taylor was more than a president; he was an icon.

On Friday, July 12, the president's body lay in state in the East Room of the White House for public viewing. The next day, Saturday, the formal funeral was held. At sunrise, guns from the various military installations around Washington began firing salutes, and an estimated one hundred thousand people thronged the streets to witness the funeral procession. The rites in the East Room were conducted by Reverend Smith Payne, the rector of St. John's Episcopal Church, and Reverend C. B. Butler, chaplain of the Senate. President Fillmore and his cabinet sat at one end of the casket and the clergy at the other. On one side of the bier sat the pallbearers and all the male members of the family, including Senator Jefferson Davis. Members of Congress and the high-ranking military sat on the side facing the family.[7] Margaret Taylor, unable to walk and also unable to stand the strain, remained on the second floor of the White House, accompanied by Mrs. Jefferson Davis.

Shortly after 1:00 PM the ceremony was complete, and Taylor's body was borne out to the black hearse in which he was to be taken to the cemetery for temporary burial. The hearse, or catafalque, was drawn by eight perfectly matched white horses, and the procession stretched a length of two miles. The parade was put together under the supervision of General Winfield Scott, Taylor's onetime friend but later rival, who had remained in New York throughout Taylor's presidency. Scott was a genius at organization, and he was the commander of the army, which made up the backbone, though not the bulk, of the procession. Scott himself was one of the spectacles of the day, riding a magnificent steed in full dress uniform, his helmet carrying a high yellow plume. Not to be left out was Taylor's horse, Old Whitey, who was led riderless with boots backward in the stirrups as was (and is) army custom.

Margaret Taylor had no intention of having her husband's body interred in Washington;[8] it would be removed to Kentucky. She refused the offers, if not pleas, of the Frankfort City Council that Taylor be buried in the state capital. Instead she had him interred in one of the family's plantations near Louisville. It was a slow process but finally, on November 4, 1850, Old Rough and Ready was laid to rest.

Epilogue

His death was a public calamity. No man could have
been more devoted to the Union or more opposed to
the slavery agitation, and his position as a Southern man
and a slave-holder, his military reputation and his election by a majority of the people of the states would
have given him a power in the settlement of these ques-
tions which no President without these qualifications
would have possessed.

—Thomas Hart Benton

Old Bullion may have been carried away in his praise of Taylor's
innate political abilities, but he knew his politics, and he owed Taylor no such compliments. Furthermore, a great many of Taylor's
contemporaries agreed with him. At the very least, had Taylor lived
and been reelected, as seems likely, the country would have been
spared the dismal presidency of Franklin Pierce, and history could
well have been different.

Despite the conjecture over Taylor's potential for saving the
Union, however, he will still be remembered more for his exploits on
the battlefield than for the wisdom of his conduct of the presidency.
In that respect, his experience resembled the way Americans view

other U.S. "military" presidents, of which there have been only five—Washington, Jackson, Taylor, Grant, and Eisenhower in chronological order. Granted, the experiences of these men varied considerably while in the army,[1] but the very nature of the military ensured that they would have some characteristics in common. Notably, they shared a reluctance to enter the political arena in the first place, a futile ambition to stay above politics and be "president of all the people," and a tendency to be too trusting of their associates in government, most of whom they were unfamiliar with on entering office.

In person, Taylor was an enigma, causing opinions of him to vary widely. Dangerous as it is to theorize on such matters, it seems possible that this inconsistency in Taylor's makeup stemmed from the fact that Taylor actually lived two lives. In one life he was born to privilege, a civilian planter, in which pursuit he was uniformly successful. He was blessed with a happy home life. His wife, Margaret, was devoted to him and, despite a genteel upbringing, bore the hardships of small posts on the frontier, so much so that Taylor once remarked, "She was a better soldier than I." That aspect of Taylor's life brought out his gentler side.

Taylor's military career, however, was a different story. Until the Mexican War made him a national hero, it was disappointing. Men such as Alexander Macomb, Winfield Scott, Edmund P. Gaines, and John E. Wool spent the years between the War of 1812 and the Mexican War as general officers or colonels. Taylor, equally deserving, was reduced from the rank of major to captain after the War of 1812 and resigned in a pique. Reinstated after a year, his journey from major to colonel (with a brevet rank of brigadier general) was long and arduous. The contrast between Taylor's two lives—civilian and military—doubtless had an effect on him. He seemed suspicious of his fellows who shared his life's calling.

Circumstances have contributed much to our inability to understand Taylor better as president. His personal papers, unfortunately, were lost during the Civil War when Union soldiers destroyed the home of Taylor's son at Baton Rouge. Richard Taylor was a major general in the Confederate Army, and he had stored his father's papers in that ill-fated mansion. The Union soldiers presumably had no idea that they were depriving history of priceless letters and documents.

And Taylor's time in office was short. He had served in the White House for only sixteen months before his untimely death, and his tenure occurred during a time of political turmoil and passion, where the critical battles were being fought in Congress. As a result, the only cause Taylor espoused that came to fruition before he died was the signing of the Clayton-Bulwer Treaty between the United States and Britain, a matter that fell exclusively in the executive purview. The issues of California statehood, settling the boundary dispute between Texas and New Mexico, and statehood for New Mexico on the basis of local sovereignty, all of which Taylor had recommended in his State of the Union address in December 1849, were still matters of violent controversy.

Soon after Taylor's death, however, these issues were solved, though only temporarily, by the enactment of a series of five laws known collectively as the Compromise of 1850. The compromise's provisions were nearly identical to those proposed earlier in the year by Henry Clay and embodied in a single measure, known at that time as the omnibus bill. That effort had been doomed to defeat; there were enough men with strong feelings about one issue or another who would vote against approving the entire package.

After much conferring, and driven by a deep desire for a compromise, younger heads on Capitol Hill, led by Senator Stephen A. Douglas of Illinois and joined by Daniel Webster, decided to submit each provision for a vote individually. President Fillmore sympathized with the effort and, once Congress approved the five separate bills, he signed them all, completing the process on September 20, 1850.

The laws together provided for (a) the admission of California as a free state, (b) the abolition of the slave trade (though not slavery itself) in the District of Columbia, (c) the admission of New Mexico and Utah as territories with popular sovereignty as to slavery,

(d) the stringent Fugitive Slave Act, and (e) the payment of $19 million to Texas for giving up its claims to western lands.

The Compromise of 1850 would probably never have become law, at least in the form that it passed, had Zachary Taylor lived, for it is generally conceded that he would have vetoed some of its provisions, particularly the Fugitive Slave Act. What would have happened then must remain as one of those imponderable might-have-beens of history.

Presidents are inevitably remembered far less for the abilities of the men occupying the office than for the magnitude of the events that happened during their administrations. Sometimes mediocre men are given undeserved status because significant events transpired during their presidencies, whereas very capable men are often overlooked because no great events happened during their terms in office.[2] Taylor fell into the second category and therefore has been generally underrated as a president.

Such judgments, however, are relatively unimportant. For Taylor deserves to be remembered for something more important: he was a man of the Union, one who placed the interests of the Union as a whole above that of his own section of the country. Perhaps, as a lifelong military man, that trait is to be expected, but in fact that is a false assumption. Witness the choice, as the Union was breaking up with the coming Civil War, made by lifelong military officers with outstanding records of service to the Union, men such as Robert E. Lee, Albert and Joseph Johnston, Pierre Beauregard, Stonewall Jackson, and many others. Taylor was truly the exception rather than the rule.[3]

Zachary Taylor was a great American, and the pages of our history are richer for the life of Old Rough and Ready.

Notes

1. EARLY CAREER

1. Holman Hamilton, *Zachary Taylor: Soldier of the Republic* (Indianapolis: Bobbs-Merrill, 1941), p. 25.
2. Ibid., p. 27.
3. K. Jack Bauer, *Zachary Taylor: Soldier, Planter, Statesman of the Old Southwest* (Baton Rouge: Louisiana State University Press, 1985), p. 6. He quotes a letter from Taylor to his father: "The people appear to be more averse to a military life in this part of the country than at Louisville or any other place that I have ever yet been at."
4. Edward M. Coffman, *The Old Army: A Portrait of the American Army in Peacetime, 1784–1898* (New York: Oxford University Press, 1986), p. 31.
5. Hamilton, *Soldier of the Republic*, p. 36.
6. Ibid., p. 37.
7. Gallatin to his wife, July 7, 1802, quoted in Coffman, *The Old Army*, p. 3.
8. See Coffman, *The Old Army*, p. 31.

2. UNSUNG HERO

1. Bauer, *Zachary Taylor*, pp. 10–11.
2. Winnebagoes, Pottawatomies, and Kickapoos.
3. The British government, its hands full fighting Napoleon, refused to recognize the state of war with the United States until December of that year, though hostilities were very real.
4. Bauer, *Zachary Taylor*, p. 11, says that Taylor was forced to pay

fifty-nine dollars, a tidy sum in those days, out of his own pocket in order to make this move.

5. Benson J. Lossing, *The Pictorial Field-Book of the War of 1812* (New York: Benchmark, 1970), p. 317.

6. Ibid.

7. Hamilton, *Soldier of the Republic*, p. 43.

8. Ibid., pp. 43–44.

9. Ibid., p. 49. Edited to modern spelling, etc. Howard later died of the fever that had prevented him from making the expedition.

10. Ibid., pp. 50–54.

11. Hamilton describes Anderson as "a crotchety old woman of a soldier" and he is even more critical of Wilkinson, calling him "a chicken-hearted fellow who tried to thwart Taylor at every step." Ibid., pp. 54–55.

12. Jonathan Jenkins, future governor of Indiana, Colonel Richard Johnson, future vice president of the United States, General Hopkins, and Representative Stephen Ormsby. Ibid., p. 56.

13. Ibid.

14. Bauer, *Zachary Taylor*, p. 17.

3. OLD ROUGH AND READY

1. Hamilton, *Soldier of the Republic*, p. 59.

2. Bauer, *Zachary Taylor*, p. 29.

3. Ibid., p. 30.

4. The hostess, the wife of ex-senator John Brown, wrote her son the next day, "The President, James Monroe, has arrived and departed. Yesterday breakfasted with us in company with General Jackson and that hero whose cool, determined, and successful courage has never been rivalled in modern time, . . . Major Zachary Taylor." Hamilton, *Soldier of the Republic*, p. 65. As a loyal Kentuckian, Mrs. Brown certainly had her priorities right.

5. The two other daughters, Ann and Sarah Know, survived. This account is taken from Ibid., pp. 65–68.

6. Oddly one account makes Black Hawk about six feet tall. Another describes him as standing only five foot four inches. Suffice it to say that he gave the appearance of height because of his personality and peculiar headdress.

7. Taylor to General Thomas Jesup, December 4, 1832, Taylor Papers, Library of Congress.

8. The term "Stillman's Run" is a complete coincidence in that the location had nothing to do with the Illinois commander.

9. Hamilton, *Soldier of the Republic*, p. 92.

10. Ibid., p. 95.
11. Ibid., p. 97.
12. John K. Mahon, *History of the Second Seminole War, 1835–1842*, rev. ed. (Gainesville: University Press of Florida, 1985), pp. 226–27.
13. Ibid., p. 227.
14. Ibid., p. 228.

4. FORT JESUP TO THE RIO GRANDE

1. K. Jack Bauer, *The Mexican War, 1846–1848* (New York: Macmillan, 1974), p. 97.
2. George Meade, *The Life and Letters of George Gordon Meade, Major-General, United States Army*, vol. 1 (New York: Charles Scribner's Sons, 1913), p. 26.
3. Samuel E. Chamberlain, *My Confession: The Recollections of a Rogue* (New York: Harper Brothers, 1956), pp. 140–41.
4. Ethan Allen Hitchcock, *Fifty Years in Camp and Field*, ed. W. A. Croffut (New York: G. P. Putnam's Sons, 1909), pp. 200–201.
5. The Mexican state of New Mexico included territories that became the states of New Mexico, Arizona, Nevada, Colorado, and parts of Utah.
6. Marcy to Taylor, January 13, 1846, U.S. Congress, House of Representatives, Executive Document no. 60, 30th Cong., 1st sess., *Messages of the President of the United States* . . . (Washington, D.C.: Wendell and Van Benthuysen, 1848), p. 91.
7. John S. D. Eisenhower, *So Far from God: The U.S. War with Mexico, 1846–1848* (New York: Random House, 1989), p. 53.
8. The *Porpoise*, the *Lawrence*, and the *Woodbury*.

5. WAR WITH MEXICO!

1. E. Kirby Smith, *To Mexico with Scott: Letters of Ephraim Kirby Smith to His Wife* (Cambridge: Harvard University Press, 1917), p. 34. Smith does not tell how the Mexican sentries made their displeasure known, whether by shouting or by firing warning shots.
2. Taylor to Wood, September 3, 1846, Executive Document no. 60, p. 6.
3. Eisenhower, *So Far from God*, pp. 66–68. The exact words were those of the Washington *Union*, Polk's newspaper organ.
4. The congressmen who voted against war were led by former president John Quincy Adams. They came to be known as the "Immortal Fourteen."
5. Brown was a fifty-eight-year-old officer from New England. His

garrison was supported by two artillery batteries, totaling eight guns. One of the batteries had four large eighteen-pounders. The other, under Captain Braxton Bragg, had three six-pounders and a mortar. That defense should be more than adequate. Eisenhower, *So Far from God*, p. 72.

6. Ibid., p. 74.
7. Executive Order no. 58, May 7, 1846, Executive Document no. 60.
8. Taylor to the adjutant general, May 9, 1846. Executive Document no. 60, pp. 296–97. Meade, *Life and Letters of George Gordon Meade*, letter, May 15, 1846, p. 83.

6. MONTERREY

1. Gaines had actually recruited 12,600 men, most of them for an illegal term of six months instead of the three months allowed by law. He sent off the 8,000 before Washington could stop him.
2. The militia were on a different status than the volunteers. The Constitution at least provides an excuse for militia to refuse deployment outside the United States.
3. It is natural to assume that Monterrey would lie to the south. However, it lies on almost exactly the same latitude as Matamoros.
4. One of them was Gideon Pillow of Tennessee, a former law partner of President Polk's who considered himself to be the "eyes and ears" of the president. The other two were Thomas L. Hamer and James Shields.
5. Taylor's low opinion of Worth's character, which may not always have been consistent, did not alter his judgment that Worth, with all his faults, was the best officer he had for independent action.
6. Because Taylor had an equal number of regulars and volunteers—and since he had two regular and only one volunteer division—he periodically attached some volunteers to the regulars. It was a source of pride to Kenly that the Baltimore Battalion, as it was commonly called, was brigaded with a regular unit in Twiggs's Division. The battalion was even issued "regular-style" blue uniforms.

7. BUENA VISTA

1. F. N. Scott to Butler, January 3, 1847, Executive Document no. 60, p. 852.
2. On December 22, 1944, when the 101st Airborne Division was surrounded by Germans, McAuliffe answered a demand for surrender by that single word.
3. Justin H. Smith, *The War with Mexico*, vol. 1 (1919; repr. Gloucester, Mass.: Peter Smith, 1963), p. 396. It seems likely that many of the

deserters would later return, because the wilds of northern Mexico do not provide many incentives for those who wished to live off the civilian economy.

8. THE ELECTION OF 1848

1. It is also noteworthy that both Scott and MacArthur, when the crunch came, placed their military duties unquestioningly above their political ambitions. MacArthur had presidential ambitions in the 1930s, even before World War II.
2. Taylor to Crittenden, January 26, 1847, cited in Mrs. Chapman Coleman, *The Life of John J. Crittenden*, vol. 1 (Philadelphia: J. B. Lippincott, 1873), p. 277.
3. Holman Hamilton, *Zachary Taylor: Soldier in the White House* (Indianapolis: Bobbs-Merrill, 1951), p. 38. The Native Americans referred to an all-white, ultraconservative party, not to the American Indian, which is now the case.
4. He was first defeated in 1824, and when convinced of defeat he threw his support to John Quincy Adams. He was defeated in 1832 against Andrew Jackson and then again, very barely, against James K. Polk in 1844. The Whigs had passed him over in favor of William Henry Harrison in 1840.
5. Hamilton, *Soldier in the White House*, p. 44.
6. Ibid., p. 13.
7. This account comes from ibid., pp. 77–81.
8. Bauer, *Zachary Taylor*, pp. 235–36.
9. Hamilton, *Soldier in the White House*, p. 95.
10. See ibid., p. 337. He uses the word "probably."
11. Ibid., pp. 137–38.
12. Ibid., p. 120.
13. Ibid., p. 132.

9. INAUGURATION AND EARLY DAYS IN THE WHITE HOUSE

1. Up until 1937, Inauguration Day was March 4. In that year it was moved to January 20.
2. James K. Polk, *Polk: The Diary of a President, 1845–1849*, ed. Allan Nevins (London: Longmans, Green, 1929), p. 362.
3. Hamilton, *Soldier in the White House*, p. 141.
4. Crittenden had served briefly as attorney general under President William Henry Harrison, who died in office after a month.
5. The State of West Virginia did not come into being until the Civil War.
6. Bauer, *Zachary Taylor*, pp. 252–53.

7. Polk, *Diary*, p. 378.
8. Ibid., p. 383.
9. For a more detailed discussion of these appointments, see Bauer, *Zachary Taylor*, pp. 260–62.
10. Polk, *Diary*, pp. 389–90.
11. Quoted in Hamilton, *Soldier in the White House*, p. 158.
12. Polk, *Diary*, p. 389.
13. Bauer, *Zachary Taylor*, p. 268.
14. Ibid., p. 269.
15. Ibid., pp. 269–70.

10. CALIFORNIA AND NEW MEXICO

1. Richard Striner, letter to author, July 7, 2007.
2. Neal Harlow, *California Conquered* (Berkeley: University of California Press, 1982), p. 281. "The results were electric. Between December 14, 1848, and January 18, 1849, sixty sailing vessels, averaging fifty passengers each, left New York, Boston, Salem, Norfolk, Philadelphia, and Baltimore for the Pacific coast. During the same period many more left New Orleans, Charleston, and other ports for the gold regions. In the month of February, 1849, sixty ships were announced to sail from New York, seventy from Philadelphia and Boston, and eleven from New Bedford. The demand for vessels was so great that ships were diverted from any other service for the purpose of accommodating those clamoring for passage to California." Cardinal Goodwin, *The Establishment of State Government in California, 1846–1850* (New York: Macmillan, 1914), p. 56.
3. "Pacific," in the *California Star*, January 22, 1848, said that California, "since the United States flag was hoisted over it, has been in a sad state of disorganization, and particularly as regards the judiciary. Indeed, sir, we have had no government at all during this period, unless the inefficient mongrel rule exercised over us be termed such."
   And in attacking the alcaldes (military-appointed town mayors), the writer asserted that they exercised "authority far greater than any officer in our republic—the president not excepted—uniting in their persons executive, legislative, and judicial functions. The grand autocrat of all the Russians . . . is the only man in Christendom I know of who equals him." Goodwin, *State Government in California*, p. 64.
4. U.S. Congress, House of Representatives, Executive Document no. 59, 31st Cong., 1st sess., *Message to the President of the United States . . .* March 27, 1850; pp. 3–4, hereafter referred to as the King Report.
5. Perhaps King's most important contribution to the matter was his detailed report of conditions in California, to include studies of soil

condition, mineral resources, agriculture, and the like. See King Report.

6. King Report, p. 6. Goodwin, *State Government in California*, pp. 84–85, contests these figures, but his objections consist of a tempest in a teapot.
7. Hamilton, *Soldier in the White House*, p. 181.
8. Ibid., p. 182.
9. Some Texans alleged that Taylor was influenced by an anti-Texan prejudice based on his disagreeable relationship with the Texas Rangers in the Mexican War. Such allegations neglect Taylor's strong support of federal over state authority.
10. Albert Castel, "Zachary Taylor," *American History Illustrated* 5, no. 3 (June 1970), p. 47.
11. It failed. New Mexico would have to wait until 1911 before gaining admission into the Union as a state.

11. FOREIGN AFFAIRS

1. Ishbel Ross, in her biography *First Lady of the South*, has left a vivid description of their dilemmas when wrestling with the decision.

   Varina [Davis] walked into the moonlit drawing room one evening and found General Narciso Lopez and an associate waiting for her husband. [Senator John] Calhoun was backing the Venezuelan-born filibuster, who was raising an expeditionary force to overthrow the government in Cuba. Lopez wished Jefferson Davis to lead the expedition and while Varina sat out of earshot, he offered to deposit $100,000 with him in his wife's name before he left, and another $100,000 or a fine coffee plantation if the expedition succeeded.

   Davis drew away, remarking proudly, "I deem it inconsistent with my duty; you must excuse me." When Varina heard what the proposal was she felt alarmed and was glad her husband had declined it. They went next to Major Robert E. Lee, who came to see Davis about the proposal, believing it would not be ethical for him to accept. This was the first time Varina and Lee met, and she considered him the handsomest person she had ever seen—"his manner, too, was the impersonation of kindness."

   Ishbel Ross, *First Lady of the South: The Life of Mrs. Jefferson Davis* (New York: Harper and Brothers, 1958), p. 59.
2. Richard Arden Wire, "John M. Clayton and the Search for Order: A Study in Whig Politics and Diplomacy" (Ph.D. diss., University of Maryland, 1971), p. 276.

3. Cornelius Vanderbilt was a part owner of this company. His partners were J. L. White and his brother David. Ibid., p. 29.
4. Hamilton, *Soldier in the White House*, p. 363.

12. THE GREAT DEBATE

1. *Calhoun, Basic Documents*, ed. John M. Anderson (State College, Penn.: Bald Eagle Press, 1952), pp. 298–324, cited in Richard Striner, *Father Abraham: Lincoln's Relentless Struggle to End Slavery* (New York: Oxford University Press, 2006), p. 27.
2. Hamilton, *Soldier in the White House*, p. 305.
3. Elbert B. Smith, *The Presidencies of Zachary Taylor and Millard Fillmore* (Lawrence: University Press of Kansas, 1988), p. 116.
4. Ibid.
5. Literally, the word means, "the Glory is departed from Israel."
6. Sarah J. Lippincott, quoted in Smith, *Presidencies*, p. 109.
7. Ibid., p. 138.
8. Ibid., p. 119.
9. Ibid., p. 120.
10. Ibid., p. 122.

13. THE DEATH OF THE PRESIDENT

1. It was noted that Galphin's rejection was doubly unjust because that worthy had performed more service in keeping the Indian quiescent than those who were paid. Smith, *Presidencies*, p. 124.
2. Hamilton, *Soldier in the White House*, p. 346.
3. Smith, *Presidencies*, p. 156.
4. Dr. Alexander Wotherspoon and Dr. Richard Coolidge of the army, Dr. Robert Wood, and Dr. James Hall, a civilian physician from Washington.
5. Smith, *Presidencies*, p. 157.
6. Hamilton, *Soldier in the White House*, pp. 393–94.
7. Bauer, *Zachary Taylor*, pp. 317–18.
8. Arlington Cemetery was not established until the Civil War, when it was appropriated from the estate of Confederate General Robert E. Lee.

EPILOGUE

1. In chapter 8, I have counted only three—Taylor, Grant, and Eisenhower. Washington was on active service for only about a dozen years. Andrew Jackson was primarily a lawyer and politician who

spent some nine years in uniform. Nevertheless, these two men made their reputations in battle.

2. It was said of Antoninus Pius, one of the "good" Roman emperors, "Happy are they whose annals are few."

3. Only a few, including Winfield Scott and George Thomas, both of Virginia, stayed with the Union—and both paid for so doing in the eyes of their former friends and families.

Milestones

1784   Born in Orange County, Virginia, on November 24. Taken by his parents to Louisville, Kentucky, at the age of a few months.

1808   Commissioned first lieutenant, Seventh Infantry Regiment.

1812   Defense of Fort Harrison, a critical post on the Wabash, elevates Taylor to the status of a public figure.

1815   Angry and disappointed over perceived lack of recognition for his services, resigns from the army. Returns to plantation at Louisville.

1816   Reenters army and accepts commission as major in command of a regiment. Keeps plantations and leads dual life.

1820   Tragedy hits. Two small daughters succumb to malaria. Wife, Margaret, survives but remains semi-invalid the rest of her life.

1832   Black Hawk War. Taylor commands all regular troops at Fort Armstrong, Rock Island, Illinois. Does not participate in any major battle.

1835   Tragedy hits again. Daughter Sarah dies of malaria three months after her marriage to Jefferson Davis, a union of which Taylor disapproves. Taylor and Davis bitterly alienated until the Mexican War. They then become allies, and Davis becomes an unofficial member of the family.

1837   Seminole War. Taylor's victory at battle of Lake Okeechobee earns him coveted promotion to brevet brigadier general.

1845   On April 7 Polk sends orders placing Taylor in command of the Corps (later Army) of Observation at Fort Jesup, on the Sabine River, ready to defend Texas against Mexico. Taylor's Army of Observation is delivered by ship on July 25 to Corpus Christi, on the Nueces River. Over a stay of eight months, Taylor trains army of 3,550 men.

1846   Taylor's army arrives at the Rio Grande on March 28 at the site of present-day Brownsville, Texas.

The Mexican War begins on April 26, precipitated by a report by Taylor of a Mexican raid across the Rio Grande into territory claimed by both Mexico and the United States.

Taylor removes threat to Texas. Victories at Palo Alto and Resaca de la Palma, near Brownsville, raise Mexican threat against Texas.

Taylor seizes Monterrey in three bloody days of fighting on September 21–23. President James K. Polk disapproves of Taylor's truce, made in the face of previous orders forbidding it. Beginning of Taylor's disenchantment with Polk.

1847   Battle of Buena Vista on February 22–23. Taylor's green army of volunteers barely survives battle against Santa Anna's attack at a point south of Saltillo, Mexico. Taylor's last battle.

Taylor returns to the United States from Mexico on December 2 to find himself a leading prospect for the presidency.

1848   Taylor writes a politically motivated letter to his brother-in-law, Captain J. S. Allison, declaring himself a good Whig, thereby making his nomination by that party a virtual certainty.

Taylor receives Whig nomination for president at Philadelphia convention on June 9.

Taylor elected president of the United States over Democrat Lewis Cass on November 7.

1849   Taylor inaugurated the twelfth president of the United States on March 5.

Visit to Pennsylvania in August and September, partly to escape cholera epidemic in Washington. Afflicted by illness, Taylor cuts the trip short.

State of the Union address outlines Taylor's proposals, led by statehood for California.

1850   Tensions with Britain over the Caribbean. Secretary of State Clayton and British representative Sir Henry Lytton Bulwer open negotiations in Washington over rights to construct a canal across Nicaragua.

Great debate in Congress over set of slavery-related issues: California statehood; Texas–New Mexico border; proposed statehood for New Mexico and Deseret (Utah); and Fugitive Slave Act.

Spirit of compromise takes hold. Senator Daniel Webster's famed Seventh of March Speech sets the groundwork for the later Compromise of 1850, sponsored by Senator Henry Clay.

Galphin scandal breaks, casting a pall over the Taylor administration.

Taylor overexerts in July 4 ceremonies and takes sick. Contracts a mysterious infection.

Taylor, unaware of the severity of his illness, signs Clayton-Bulwer Treaty with Britain, his last official act.

Death of President Zachary Taylor on July 9, surrounded by his family.

Selected Bibliography

BOOKS

Alcaraz, Ramon, et al. *The Other Side: Notes for the History of the War Between Mexico and the United States.* Translated from the Spanish and edited by Albert C. Ramsey. New York: John Wiley, 1850.

Barbour, Philip and Martha. *The Journals of Major Philip Norbourne Barbour and His Wife Martha Isabella Hopkins Barbour.* Edited by Rhoda Van Bibber Tanner Doubleday. New York: G. P. Putnam's Sons, 1936.

Bauer, K. Jack. *The Mexican War, 1846–1848.* New York: Macmillan, 1974.

———. *Zachary Taylor: Soldier, Planter, Statesman of the Old Southwest.* Baton Rouge: Louisiana State University Press, 1985.

Benton, Senator Thomas Hart. *Thirty Years' View; or A History of the Working of the American Government for Thirty Years, from 1820 to 1850.* 2 vols. New York: D. Appleton, 1854.

Calhoun, John C. *Correspondence of John C. Calhoun.* Edited by J. Franklin Jameson. Vol. 2, Annual Report of the American Historical Association, 1899. Washington: American Historical Association, 1900.

Chaffin, Tom. *Fatal Glory: Narciso López and the First Clandestine U.S. War Against Cuba.* Charlottesville: University Press of Virginia, 1996.

Chamberlain, Samuel E. *My Confession: The Recollections of a Rogue.* New York: Harper Brothers, 1956.

Coffman, Edward M. *The Old Army: A Portrait of the American Army in Peacetime, 1784–1898.* New York: Oxford University Press, 1986.

Coleman, Mrs. Chapman. *The Life of John J. Crittenden, with Selections from His Correspondence and Speeches.* 2 vols. Philadelphia: J. B. Lippincott, 1873.

Colton, Calvin. *The Life and Times of Henry Clay.* 2 vols. New York: A. S. Barnes, 1845.

Eisenhower, John S. D. *So Far from God: The U.S. War with Mexico, 1846–1848.* New York: Random House, 1989.

Eliot, Charles W. *Winfield Scott: The Soldier and the Man.* New York: Macmillan, 1937.

Fry, J. Reese. *A Life of Zachary Taylor, Comprising a Narrative of Events Connected with His Professional Career.* Philadelphia: Grigg, Elliot, 1848.

Giddings, Luther. *Sketches of the Campaign in Northern Mexico in Eighteen Hundred Forty-six and Seven.* New York: George P. Putnam, 1853.

Goodwin, Cardinal. *The Establishment of State Government in California, 1846–1850.* New York: Macmillan, 1914.

Grant, Ulysses Simpson. *Personal Memoirs of U. S. Grant,* vol. 1. New York: Charles A. Webster, 1885.

Hamilton, Holman. *Zachary Taylor: Soldier in the White House.* Indianapolis: Bobbs-Merrill, 1951.

———. *Zachary Taylor: Soldier of the Republic.* Indianapolis: Bobbs-Merrill, 1941.

Harlow, Neal. *California Conquered.* Berkeley: University of California Press, 1982.

Hitchcock, Ethan Allen. *Fifty Years in Camp and Field.* Edited by W. A. Croffut. New York: G. P. Putnam's Sons, 1909.

Holt, Michael F. *The Rise and Fall of the American Whig Party.* New York: Oxford University Press, 1999.

Lossing, Benson J. *The Pictorial Field-Book of the War of 1812.* New York: Benchmark, 1970.

Mahon, John K. *History of the Second Seminole War, 1835–1842.* Rev. ed. Gainesville: University Press of Florida, 1985.

Meade, George G. *The Life and Letters of George Gordon Meade, Major-General, United States Army.* New York: Charles Scribner's Sons, 1913.

Nevins, Allan. *The Ordeal of the Union,* vol. 1. New York: Charles Scribner's Sons, 1947.

Polk, James K. *Polk: The Diary of a President, 1845–1849.* Edited by Allan Nevins. London: Longmans Green, 1929.

Potter, David M. *The Impending Crisis, 1848–1861.* New York: Harper and Row, 1976.

Ross, Ishbel. *First Lady of the South: The Life of Mrs. Jefferson Davis.* New York: Harper and Brothers, 1958.

Scott, Winfield. *The Memoirs of Lieut-Gen Winfield Scott, LLD.* 2 vols. New York: Sheldon, 1864.

Smith, Elbert B. *The Presidencies of Zachary Taylor and Millard Fillmore.* Lawrence: University Press of Kansas, 1988.

Smith, E. Kirby. *To Mexico with Scott: Letters of Ephraim Kirby Smith to His Wife.* Cambridge: Harvard University Press, 1917.

Smith, Justin H. *The Annexation of Texas.* New York: AMS Press, 1971. Reprint from the 1911 edition, New York.

————. *The War with Mexico.* 2 vols. Gloucester, Mass.: Peter Smith, 1963. Originally published 1919 by Macmillan.

Striner, Richard. *Father Abraham: Lincoln's Relentless Struggle to End Slavery.* New York: Oxford University Press, 2006.

Taylor, Zachary. *Letters of Zachary Taylor from the Battlefields of the Mexican War.* Rochester, N.Y.: William K. Bixby, 1908. Reprint, New York: Krause Reprint Company, 1970.

Upton, Brevet Major General Emory. *The Military Policy of the United States.* Fourth Impression. Washington, D.C.: Government Printing Office, 1917. First manuscript, 1881.

U.S. Congress. House of Representatives. Executive Document No. 59. 30th Cong., 1st sess. *Correspondence Between the Secretary of War and General Scott.* Washington, D.C., 1848.

U.S. Congress. House of Representatives. Executive Document No. 60. 30th Cong., 1st sess. *Messages of the President of the United States with the Correspondence, Therewith Communicated, Between the Secretary of War and Other Officers of the Government: The Mexican War.* Washington, D.C., Wendell and Van Benthuysen, 1848.

Webb, Walter Prescott. *The Texas Rangers in the Mexican War.* Austin: Jenkins Garrett Press, 1975.

ARTICLES

Castel, Albert. "Zachary Taylor." *American History Illustrated* 5, no. 3, (June 1970).

UNPUBLISHED MANUSCRIPTS

U.S. Congress. House of Representatives. Executive Document No. 59, 31st Cong., 1st sess. *Message to the President of the United States. The Report of T. Butler King, Esq., heretofore appointed bearer of despatches and special agent to California.* March 27, 1850.

Wire, Richard Arden. "John M. Clayton and the Search for Order: A Study in Whig Politics and Diplomacy." Ph.D. diss., University of Maryland, 1971.

Acknowledgments

My wife, Joanne, is always at the top of the list of those who make my books possible. Her involvement in this biography is a bit less than in the other books because she is immersed in writing her own book about President Woodrow Wilson and his times. However, in her researches at the National Archives and Library of Congress, she has always kept an eye out for items pertaining to Zachary Taylor, and she passes them on. In this she was generously assisted by Jeffrey M. Flannery, head of the Manuscript Division, Library of Congress. And not to be ignored is her tolerance of the traumas that any book brings to a household.

Louis D. Rubin Jr., Distinguished Professor of English Emeritus at the University of North Carolina, very generously went over the entire manuscript, as he has done with my other books, and caught me with some real bloopers. I have come to rely on him not only for double-checking but for assurances.

Dorothy (Dodie) Yentz, as always, is the person who makes my books possible, and this one is no exception. Her knowledge of English mechanics, her keen eye, and remarkable expertise in computers have taken months off the production of this book.

Others have been helpful as well. Mr. Rodney A. Ross, of the National Archives, produced a hard-to-find report on the King mission to California, for which I am grateful.

Mitchell Yockelson, also of the National Archives, is my backup in that organization and never hesitates to help in any request. Among other contributions, he guided me to Rodney Ross, mentioned above.

Professor Sean Wilentz, the general editor of this series, and Paul Golob, the editorial director of Times Books, were unusually helpful, especially in dealing with the political issues of Taylor's presidency.

Dr. Richard Striner, professor of history at Washington College, Chestertown, Maryland, kindly took the time to look over critical chapters on American politics, much to my benefit.

Chris Robinson. Although this book required only one map, Chris, the cartographer on previous books, lent his usual zeal and expertise, for which I am grateful.

Index

Note: ZT stands for Zachary Taylor throughout this index

ABOUT THE AUTHOR

JOHN S. D. EISENHOWER is a retired brigadier general, U.S. Army Reserve, a former U.S. ambassador to Belgium, and the author of numerous works of military history and biography, including *General Ike: A Personal Reminiscence, They Fought at Anzio, Yanks: The Epic Story of the American Army in World War I, The Bitter Woods,* and *So Far from God: The U.S. War with Mexico, 1846–1848.* He lives in Maryland.